REAL LIVES of TEACHERS

REAL LIVES of TEACHERS

NAVIGATING THE HIGHS & LOWS OF SCHOOLS TODAY

Emma Kell

S Sage

1 Oliver's Yard
55 City Road
London EC1Y 1SP

2455 Teller Road
Thousand Oaks
California 91320

10th Floor, Emaar Capital Tower 2
MG Road, Sikanderpur, Sector 26
Gurugram, Haryana – 122002
India

8 Marina View Suite 43-053
Asia Square Tower 1
Singapore 018960

Editor: Amy Thornton
Editorial assistant: Harry Dixon
Production editor: Sarah Cooke
Marketing manager: Dilhara Attygalle
Cover design: Wendy Scott
Typeset by: C&M Digitals (P) Ltd, Chennai, India
Printed in the UK by Bell & Bain Ltd, Glasgow
BB0357847

Library of Congress Control Number: 2025937979

British Library Cataloguing in Publication Data

A catalogue record for this book is available from the British Library

ISBN 978-1-5296-8110-9 (pbk)
ISBN 978-1-5296-8111-6

This book is for the difference-makers. You are seen, you are heard and you are appreciated.

TABLE OF CONTENTS

ABOUT THE AUTHOR

Emma Kell is a teacher, keynote speaker, coach and author. She is director of Those That Can Ltd and has 26 years of experience as a teacher and leader in UK schools. Through Those That Can, she works with professionals within the world of education to provide research-based, practical sessions to promote wellbeing and effectiveness and stakeholder engagement. She is a qualified Performance Coach and experienced speaker and facilitator. Emma is an established voice in teacher wellbeing in the UK and has a growing international reputation, working with policy-makers from the World Bank and as a thought leader for OECD. She has completed a doctorate on teacher wellbeing and parenting at Middlesex University and is author of *How To Survive in Teaching* (Bloomsbury, 2018), *A Little Guide For Teachers: Wellbeing and Self-Care* and *A Little Guide for Teachers: Engaging Parents and Carers*. She is wife to a journalist and mum to two teenagers and a golden retriever called Rebel. She can be found at www.those-that-can.com/.

ABOUT THE AUTHOR

ACRONYMS

The world of teaching is fraught with acronyms. I've attempted to keep these to a minimum, but have provided below a guide to some of those that arise in this UK context.

ADHD: Attention Deficit Hyperactivity Disorder

AHT: Assistant Headteacher

ASD: Autism Spectrum Disorder

CPD: Continuing Professional Development

ECT: Early Career Teacher

EEF: Education Endowment Foundation

HR: Human Resources

ISI: Independent Schools Inspectorate

LSA: Learning Support Assistant

MFL: Modern Foreign Languages

NAHT: National Association of Headteachers

NASENCo: National Awards for Special Needs Coordination

NFER: National Federation for Education Research

NPQSL: National Professional Qualification for Senior Leadership

NQT: Newly Qualified Teacher

PPA: Planning, Preparation and Assessment

PSHE: Personal, Social, Health and Economic Education

SCITT: School-Centred Initial Teacher Training

SDP: School Development Plan

SEND: Special Educational Needs and Disabilities

SENDCo: Special Educational Needs Coordinator

SLT: Senior Leadership Team

TA: Teaching Assistant

FOREWORD

I remember when I retrained to become a teacher back in 2010. It was one of the proudest moments of my life. There was something special about knowing I was a qualified teacher, and I couldn't wait to let everyone know. When out with friends and meeting new people, I couldn't wait for the inevitable, 'So, what do you do?' question. 'I'm a primary school teacher', I would reply proudly. Fifteen years on, where I now have what you'd call a portfolio-career (I teach, lecture, write, deliver training), I still mostly identify as being a teacher, first and foremost. It's what makes all the other roles in my work make sense. Becoming a teacher changed how I viewed myself.

Reading Emma's deeply reflective book has allowed me to revisit those feelings of pride and purpose, and it will do the same for you. Emma starts by asking you to reflect on why you chose to become an educator. Knowing your 'reason for getting out of bed in the morning', or Ikigai as the Japanese refer to it, is crucially important. Having a strong sense of purpose in life is linked with better health, longevity and happiness. Too often though, we may start our careers with a clear reason for why we chose to do this job but we may end up in roles or on paths that no longer feel aligned to our original sense of purpose. So, whether you are starting out in education, or decades into a long career, Emma's writing will help you reflect on where you are and how to get to where you want to be.

I love how this book doesn't sugar-coat the experience of real educators. Teaching is hard. It comes with a lot of stresses and challenges that many people outside of education fail to understand. My wife, a senior marketing manager who has worked at large, multi-national companies, once volunteered to read one afternoon with children in my Year 2 class. She was in bed that evening by 8pm. Teaching can be draining and all-consuming which is why Emma bangs the drum for boundaries and support networks. Teaching is not a solo sport but a team game. We need good people around us, inside and outside of school to support us when the you-know-what hits the fan. Sickness, bereavement, global pandemics, war... these cataclysmic events affect us all directly and indirectly. In this book, you'll hear from educators who have gone through dark times and how they came out the other side. Emma shares their stories with grace and a sense of optimism and hope.

And of course, Emma dedicates a whole chapter to the topic of joy – how to seek it out and cultivate it. Working with children and young people, at the same time as being incredibly challenging at times, can also be immeasurably rewarding and joyful! I have lost count of the number of times I have laughed in class when a child has done or said something unexpectedly funny. However, all too often, we gloss over or forget those moments. Emma talks about how our 'negativity bias' means our brains are wired to pay more attention to the bad stuff (so we can avoid dangers and ultimately survive) than the good. This book coaches you in noticing and savouring those joyful moments. It is such an important skill and will support you in enjoying a long and satisfying career in education.

Finally, I just want to end on a philosophical note. Roughly 2,500 years ago, scribed on the entrance of the Temple of Apollo, were the immortal words, 'Know Thyself'. It was a maxim attributed to Socrates who believed the most important thing we can do, in order to lead a 'good life', is to thoroughly examine our lives, to delve into our minds and hearts, to understand our desires and motivations, to reflect on our strengths and our weaknesses and examine what kind of life we want to lead. I believe this is what Emma's brilliant book does – it helps you to know yourself.

I hope you enjoy this book as much as I did. It will make you laugh. It may make you cry. Most of all, it will help you reflect on who you are and what type of educator (and human being) you want to be.

Adrian Bethune

Adrian is a part-time teacher at a primary school in Aylesbury, Associate Lecturer at Oxford Brookes University, Deputy Chair of the Well Schools strategic board and the founder of Teachappy: www.teachappy.co.uk. Socials: @Adrianbethune.

INTRODUCTION

BEGINNINGS

Let's picture it: you're in your very own classroom, with your photo of your dog/child/ favourite view on the desk to keep you grounded, your compulsory snacks (because it's hungry work) in your bottom drawer and you're in your best teacher outfit. Your glue sticks are still smugly moist, with lids intact, and in a few months you will wonder at how you once had access to working, multi-coloured board pens. You've painstakingly planned your lesson, including several iterations depending on the weather, mood of the children and whatever might have happened in the corridor on their way. You've reminded them of your ground rules, set out the task, explained it again, used your best version of dual coding (or equivalent) to make sure they all understand, invited questions, cold-called (or equivalent) to check for understanding. Attention levels are where you need them to be; all instructions have been repeated, modelled, and scaffolded using all of the tools in your rather overflowing toolkit. 'Right, off you go!' you say. A few students continue to stare at you. You give it time and a few gentle prompts and reminders. Minutes later, a handful are yet to pick up their pens.

'But *Miss!*' one says. 'How do I *start?*'

You turn to the board to share your frustration with an inanimate object, reminding yourself of the expected teacher standards for professional conduct, take a deep breath, and turn back to start again.

As I embark on this new book, my empathy for our baffled (or 'baff-ed' – teenage slang is one of my favourite things) young people is high. Let's zoom out for a moment and head back to basics...

WHO AM I TO WRITE THIS BOOK?

This isn't an autobiographical book, though I will pepper it with some of my own observations from my 25 years in schools, so I'll keep this bit brief. I write with optimism and pragmatism. I bring to this book an acute first- and second-hand awareness of the challenges facing educators combined with a profound sense of loyalty to our vulnerable yet precious profession. I bring curiosity about and fascination with the stories of those working in schools. The power of these stories is huge and what readers take away from them will be unique to their situation but, I believe, precious and powerful.

I AM A TEACHER

I've had a blessedly happy career with a few challenging periods from which I've learned loads about myself and the profession. Starting my teacher training in 1998, I've held roles from teaching assistant to middle leader and senior leader, specialising in MFL and later in English. Much of my career has been spent in inner-London, working at schools which led smartarse friends to remind me to pack my stab vest. For the last five years, I've been lucky enough to work in alternative provision with the children – and families – who've struggled to remain in mainstream schools. On setting up my own business, I took a few weeks out of the classroom and missed it so much that I begged a colleague to let me back in.

I AM A COACH AND RESEARCHER

I became a coach during the height of the Covid-19 pandemic, starting out by supporting headteachers as they navigated the frequently nightmarish maze of unknowns and tried to keep everyone else safe – often letting their own needs drop to the bottom of the pile. Since then, I have been uniquely privileged to have coached over 200 people working in schools. Coaching taught me not to assume, but to really *listen*. Whilst the voices of my coaches are safe behind strict codes of anonymity, their stories are with me as I write, and the stories I share help me better support each new coaching client that comes my way.

I completed my doctoral studies in teachers' work-family balance (Kell, 2016) and have researched and published three books about schools and educators, focusing on wellbeing and parental engagement (Kell, 2018; Bethune and Kell, 2020, Kell and Stewart, 2022). Through my research, writing, and most recently my coaching, I have had the profound honour of hearing stories from thousands of people working in schools. These stories form the heart and lungs of this book.

I AM A MUM

I've been surprised at how strongly my children's voices have informed this book – their comments on schools and teaching – from the scathing to the strikingly intuitive – resound alongside the voices of the thousands of young people I've been lucky enough to work with. At the time of writing, they are in the full throes of adolescence and able to cut through the nonsense and say it as they see it, at its most painful, glorious, and sometimes wildly insulting! They remind me of my boundaries like nobody else – whilst also reminding me of the power of educators and schools to shape the next generation.

I AM A WIFE AND A FRIEND

My husband isn't a teacher; he's a hard-grafting TV journalist. Why is this significant? His professional perspective helps hold up a mirror to our profession, sometimes illuminating, sometimes alarming, sometimes sobering. Over the years, there have been fierce debates over whose job is most significant or most exhausting. He's been able to help me climb down from my high horse when I fall into the trap of imagining our job is the hardest in the world, and helped me sift the ludicrous from the shocking and the resilience-building as I've navigated the ups and downs of my career. My friends include those as imbued in our education system as I am and those from very different worlds, and they too provide perspective, necessary distraction and a reminder of who I am when I get lost in the labyrinth. Their perspectives too are peppered through this book.

WHAT THIS BOOK IS... AND WHAT IT ISN'T

This germ of the idea for this book came from Mary Myatt, with her line, now widely referred to in education in the UK: 'Human beings first, professionals second' (Myatt, 2016, p.13). After all, to teach is to bring your humanity into the classroom; it's a deeply personal investment. You can't hide behind equipment or instruments – when you stand in front of a group of young people, what they see is you – or arguably a version of you – without armour. They can sense how much you care, pick up on when you're having a tough day, can see when you're frustrated or proud – so, rather than trying to repress or deny this humanity, I propose with this book that we embrace it; that we acknowledge the messiness that comes with human organisms working with other human organisms – a messiness which no number of schemes of learning, development plans or risk assessments can fully mitigate.

Is teaching 'just a job'? I've been involved in some fairly fierce debates on this subject. For some, it's a lifestyle – I recall the headteacher in my community as a child who presented as The Headteacher whenever we met her – at the fête on a Saturday, in church on a Sunday, as the willing helper with problems and issues with anything related to young people and education – and I think this probably made her happy. It was her choice, and if yours is similar – and it makes you happy, too – that's brilliant. But for most of us, we didn't choose our job as a lifestyle – we have other people and other things pulling on our attention and emotional energy. I'd suggest that we replace the word 'job' with 'vocation'. But let's bear in mind that one of the things that distinguishes working in a school from many other professions is that the job is never-ending – you could work 24 hours a day, 7 days a week, 365 days a year, and someone would still want something else from you – there would still be a lesson plan that needs improving, a resource that needs refining. This is a job with something called 'spillover', which is literally what it suggests. If we don't put dams in place, the job spills over into our thoughts, our emotions, our Saturday nights and our relationships. It's our responsibility to get reasonable boundaries that work for each of our unique situations in place. I discuss more on striking the balance between 'just a job' and 'teaching as a lifestyle' in Chapter 8, 'Life Happens'.

I'm fascinated by how our experiences (within and outside work), however apparently momentous or tiny, evoke emotions and reactions and influence how we feel about our professional roles – how they influence our effectiveness, our self-efficacy, our likelihood of staying in a school, or staying in the profession. Recruitment and retention have always been a passion of mine, and at the time of writing, the crisis in this area appears to have become a perennial issue.

As with all my work, this book is practical and based on experience and research. It doesn't shy from exploring challenges and difficulties, but overall, its message is positive – this job is survivable – and thrive-able. This book is *not* a user-manual, it doesn't take a one-size-fits-all approach, because we all show up in the world in different ways – we communicate in different ways, define and experience success in different ways, different things make us happy and different things make us vulnerable. A note on terminology – you'll note that I shift between the terms 'teacher' and 'educator' – ultimately, the word 'teacher' is used to describe all of you – the support teachers, the leaders, the pastoral staff – who work with young people.

HOW TO USE THIS BOOK

This book should be infinitely readable – you can dip in and dip out depending on which sections catch your interest, and you don't have to read it in order. But my approach to the writing and research is grounded in my academic training, particularly with regard to ethical considerations. All stories are carefully anonymised with key details changed to protect identities of individuals and schools without detracting from the essence of each story and its message.

The book is written to be interactive, so use the spaces and prompts to jot down your own thoughts (or use a separate journal). Many people find visuals powerful, so it includes various conceptual models (some mine, others from people far wiser) that I've collated over the years of working with others on their goals and their wellbeing. Many educators have generously shared their stories to provide multiple perspectives on the themes explored – these have been included as case studies and redrafted to keep identities private.

With this book, I use my voice to give voice to others. This is partly selfish – I'm insatiably curious about others' stories, but I've learned that the sharing of these stories can be extremely powerful – they reassure others that they're not alone. The stories provide alternative perspectives and multiple interpretations of what it is to be a human being and work in a school. Brilliant educators come in numerous different forms – and so do struggling educations. Ultimately, we each deserve to thrive, as well as survive in our work.

REFERENCES

Bethune, A. and Kell, E. (2020). *A little guide for teachers: Teacher wellbeing and self-care*. Sage.

Kell, E. (2016). *Shifting identities: A mixed-methods study of the experiences of teachers who are also parents* (Thesis). Middlesex University, School of Health and

Education. https://repository.mdx.ac.uk/download/1036d0ec083ce6353007738348b9b7946402df67fe8d9b5671fb5f1cbc08c831/3958117/EKellThesis.pdf

Kell, E. (2018). *How to survive in teaching: Without imploding, exploding or walking away*. Bloomsbury.

Kell, E. and Stewart, C. (2022). *A little guide for teachers: Engaging parents and carers with school*. Sage.

Myatt, M. (2016). *High challenge, low threat*. John Catt.

1

BEGINNINGS

This chapter explores:

- **Being an educator:** Exploring the essence of working in a school.
- **Authenticity in teaching:** Embracing your true self in the profession.
- **Impostor syndrome:** Tips for managing and reflecting on its implications.
- **Qualities of a great teacher:** Highlighting diverse qualities for effectiveness.
- **Kindness, compassion, and structure:** Their importance for young people.
- **Setting intentions:** Reflecting on professional goals for the term or year ahead.

MY STORY

I've always found starting afresh in a new context as overwhelming as I have exciting. A new school can feel like a brand new profession and, in my experience, absorbing the cultural norms and habits and really feeling as if you belong takes time. Invariably, there's so much to take in on the first day, from the vital safeguarding procedures to the way the curriculum is organised to how to make the interactive whiteboard work. I've often subjected myself to huge pressure to absorb it all as quickly as possible, leaving my brain buzzing with overload by the end of the first day. This chapter was quite cathartic and, I hope, homes in on what matters most.

WHAT DOES IT MEAN TO BE AN EDUCATOR? WHAT IS IT TO WORK IN A SCHOOL?

I headed out into the fresh air to do this exercise for myself. Heading out into the open air isn't always possible with a class of 30, I grant you, but I do remember heading out for several vigorous laps of the school field with a teenager on the verge of vomiting with nerves just before her German speaking exam, and it did the trick. Fresh air and exercise usually do.

Reflection: What it Means to be an Educator

What are the first things you think of when you consider the words 'teacher' and 'school'? Don't think about it too hard! Jot down some words or images in the box below.

Here are some of my thoughts, in no particular order:

- 'MUM!' (one of my teenagers – you'll hear more from them in the course of the book). 'Will you STOP being such a teacher!' (I was making conversation with a group of their friends in the car.)
- Scarves. A few years into teaching, I'd amassed a rather delightful set of scarves – scarves with owls, stars, flamingos; the more colourful the better. Met an old friend. 'Oh my goodness,' he said. 'You look like such a teacher.' (I've barely worn a scarf since.)
- The 70s, aged 4. An accidental fart and my first memory of an encounter with a teacher. 'Will you stop trailing it around!'
- 1990. Mrs S. A Level German (to this day, the hardest thing I've ever done). 'If you stretch people, they grow.' (I did – and spent a very happy year living in Berlin soon after this.)
- 1994, whilst wearing pair of clown-style dungarees of which I was particularly proud. I took it upon myself to start organising and shifting tables in the pub. 'Oh my goodness, Emma. You're such a teacher!'
- 1998. The decision to teach had made its inevitable arrival and I was out with friends. 'Emma, show us your teacher stare again!' Howls of laughter. 'You look constipated'.

EMBRACING YOUR AUTHENTIC SELF AS AN EDUCATOR

If you're reading this, I'm going to hazard that the chances are that you work – or have worked – in a school, have an interest in education or have a loved one in the field. So, let's consider your perception of yourself (or your loved one) as an educator.

Reflection: Your Motivations for Becoming an Educator

What do you bring to the profession? Consider the qualities that you are aware of in yourself and that others have reflected back to you. Consider your life experience, passions and skills. Make a few notes in the box below.

For more on you and your qualities, see the Johari window activity in Chapter 3. We delve more deeply into values later in this chapter, so you'll be able to build on this reflection.

Whilst, with a mix of pride and acute embarrassment, I have lost count of the times I've been described as 'such a teacher', 25 years into the profession, I still half expect someone to come barging into the classroom to announce that it wasn't *that* Emma Kell they'd employed and to give me my marching orders, because most of us have a gremlin that lives on our shoulder and delights in self-sabotage. On which note, it's worth getting in early with the subject of impostor syndrome, because it's widespread and, frankly, a pain in the bum – watching others apparently sail through challenges with unassailable confidence whilst we tie ourselves in knots of self-doubt is no way to live!

MANAGING IMPOSTOR SYNDROME

- Impostor syndrome is often a sign of competence rather than failure. Unlike the Dunning-Kruger effect, where people with limited ability overestimate their competence, those experiencing impostor feelings are usually more self-aware and reflective. If you're questioning your abilities, it's likely because you're genuinely engaged with your work and holding yourself to high standards.
- Try using oppositional thinking to challenge your inner critic. When you catch yourself thinking 'I'm not good enough,' respond with a thought that reflects evidence from your actual experience, such as 'I managed that difficult class situation well yesterday' or 'I've had positive feedback from students.' Actively pushing back against negative self-talk helps to break its hold.

- Impostor syndrome often stems from the brain's negativity bias. This is the tendency to focus on perceived threats and shortcomings as a way to protect ourselves. Recognising that your brain is trying to keep you safe – not necessarily tell you the truth – can help you take those thoughts less seriously and reduce their power over you.
- Talk to others about how you're feeling. Impostor thoughts can thrive in isolation, but many teachers experience them, even those who appear confident. Sharing your experiences with trusted colleagues or friends can be reassuring and normalising, helping you realise you're far from alone.
- Redefine what success looks like. Teachers often hold themselves to unrealistic standards, trying to be inspiring, organised, compassionate and innovative all at once. But perfection isn't the goal – making a positive impact is. Consider what a 'good enough' day looks like. It's likely that even on your hardest days, you're still making a difference.

Our perceptions of teachers and teaching are influenced by numerous factors, including upbringing, location, opportunities, life events, and personal challenges. But the chances of seeing ourselves, fully, congruently, as fitting into the role are slim, and it's my experience that we spend an awful lot of (wasted?) energy trying to fit ourselves into the 'ideal' mould we imagine (cue memories of trying to emulate a colleague early in my career and ending up a sobbing heap in the office).

My research and experience tells me that the reality is much simpler than we often imagine (as is so often true of life)…

THE SIMPLE TRUTH IS THAT BRILLIANT TEACHERS COME IN ALL SHAPES AND SIZES

I've had the privilege and pleasure of working with, being taught by, and seeing my daughters taught by hundreds of highly effective teachers, from the loud and flamboyant to the quiet and measured; the serious and bookish to the irreverent and hilarious; those with impeccably high standards and those who flirt with the boundaries of the acceptable; those who are suited and booted and those who flout dress-codes; those who've had disastrous starts to their careers and those who've flown through the ranks; those who've struggled with mental, physical and emotional challenges; those who are making a beeline for headship and those who see no greater reward and fulfilment than to spend their career as a teaching assistant or main scale teacher. To distil and 'bottle' what they have in common is the million-dollar question, and, as with many of the most challenging conundrums of all, I find it best to turn to children for the answer.

Firstly, it's worth noting that young people are, broadly speaking, amongst the most forgiving I've ever known. A disastrous lesson? A moment of unplanned emotion in the classroom? Acknowledge it and move on – in the vast majority of cases, they will too (cue distinct memories from early in my inner-London teaching life of being told to 'f**k off' one day and being greeted with a cheery 'Morning, Miss!' the next day).

I did a quick poll which received around 500 responses from young people via social media. It read as follows:

Hivemind, could you do me a favour and turn to the nearest under 18 (if you have one at your disposal) and ask them to complete this sentence…? A good teacher is…

I created a word cloud from the responses. The result, I thought, was both striking and quite reassuring. See if you agree.

The most frequent word to occur was: **Kind** followed by **Fun**.

After that came: **Cares**, **Good**, **Strict** and **Listen**.

Then: **Respectful**, **Help**, **Nice**, **Fair**.

Followed by:

Smart	Funny	Someone
Understanding	Enthusiastic	Knows
Books	Compliment	Learning
Helpful	Others	Stress
Give	Open-minded	Reliable
Control	Knowledgeable	Firm
Engaging	Passionate	Pushes
Teacher	Lessons	Correct
Caring	Resilient	Enthusiastic

A few points to note, but let's start with a caveat – this is very much my network and so is inevitably a skewed sample. The area is certainly worthy of further research. But for now, let's consider some of the emerging themes:

- Young people thrive on kindness and compassion – they want to know you listen in order to understand. They want to know they will receive help when they need it.
- 'Strict is often good', as my daughter often says. Most young people welcome structure (even if they don't admit it) – it makes them feel safe; it helps them

understand what is expected from them. If they know where the goalposts are, they know what success looks like.

- Young people need to feel successful. If we flip this, I'd suggest that the vast majority of behaviour problems arise from children feeling 'stupid' – as if they don't understand. This suggestion is borne out by my numerous conversations with young people in alternative provision, who have either been excluded or suspended from mainstream schools

---

Case Study: Reece

'I Felt Thick'

Reece is fifteen. Reece has been excluded from three difference schools. I'm teaching him English GCSE. We have two months to go to the final exams. He hates English, he says. Those are the only words he utters for three weeks of my lessons, and my jovial attempts to engage him with the 'cats over dogs' debate (usually a surefire success), and dozens of other creative approaches to build trust and create a relationship have fallen flat.

Reece's file makes eye-watering reading and I feel many pangs of sympathy for his mainstream teachers and peers. When he finally opens up (counter-intuitively, we used 'what I hate about schools' as the first writing task he willingly engaged in), he admits he really shouldn't have pushed that teacher, 'but he was in my face, Miss. He wouldn't stop shouting. Bro, his breath *stank* of coffee. Rank...'. He reflects back on Year 7. 'I lost my timetable and didn't know where to get a new one. I kept getting lost on the way to lessons. OK, yeah, the corridors were more fun, but... Yeah. I was always late. I couldn't sit still. I didn't get it. I didn't know what was going on in there, man. She wouldn't help me.'

This story obviously has more than one side and comes with a substantial side-serving of salt. Reece admitted his chosen mode of communication to request help was possibly suboptimal. He admitted that it wasn't the teacher's fault he'd missed the introduction, the instructions, the reminders of previous learning and the context of the lesson. But the emotions associated with that period are clearly still raw.

'I wanted to do well, Miss. Honestly. I just felt so... *thick*.'

The behaviour lead called Reece's mum in repeatedly. 'He's sabotaging the learning of others.' His mum's recollection of the period (and the many similar periods that followed) are as bitter, if not more so, than Reece's – 'they made me feel like a sh*t parent. I hated going to that school! They made it sound as if he was doing it all on purpose.'

Reece has a recent diagnosis of dyslexia, ADHD and recurring bouts of acute depression and anxiety. Like all children who land in alternative provision (settings for those unable to cope in mainstream), he had needs that were misunderstood and undiagnosed for years, and he found his own ways of muddling through and avoiding people and situations that made him vulnerable.

Postscript: With the support of a phenomenal army of dedicated specialists, Reece gradually found confidence and a sense of identity. He achieved a Grade 6 in English Language in his GCSEs and has, at the time of writing, successfully sustained a well-paid role in landscape gardening alongside his studies.

Reflection: The Qualities and Characteristics of Impactful Teachers

What were the qualities and characteristics of the teachers who shaped your life in a positive way?

What qualities do *you* want your students to experience and remember from you as a key adult in their lives?

THE ROAD TO HERE: BECOMING A TEACHER. STARTING WITH 'WHY?'

Simon Sinek's work around finding your 'why' remains a talisman in my work and life. Sinek states: 'Regardless of WHAT we do in our lives, our WHY – our driving purpose, cause or belief – never changes' (2011, p.151).

I have examined in some detail in previous books what motivates people to work in schools – check out *How to Survive in Teaching* (Kell, 2018) for a detailed examination of this subject. 'What's your why?' is one of my favourite questions of all, because it sounds so broad, but the themes that come out in the responses are powerful in their simplicity.

Difference-Making

It's about leaving the world a better place than we found it; it's about moral purpose and social imperatives. See the next section on Ikigai, where we will explore this in more detail.

Personal Experience

Some of us had a blissfully happy time at school; many of us didn't. It's about either giving our students a positive experience like the one we had or ensuring they never feel as humiliated, small or silly as perhaps we once did. My own was mainly positive, with darker moments that still inform and guide me. Being told by one teacher that I'd 'never set the world alight' has acted as fuel to prove him wrong and a pledge that no child will ever feel small or insignificant in my classroom.

Passion and Variety

Passion for our subjects – for the potential of Physics or Art or Sport to change young people's lives for the better is a big driving factor, and the 'never boring' truism about schools is also a big attraction.

Young People

To this day, I'd take a room full of hormonal teenagers over a room full of grumpy adults, any day of the week. Relishing our time with young people is a huge motivator for those working in schools.

IKIGAI

Ikigai, a Japanese concept roughly translated as a 'reason for being' or a 'direction or purpose in life' provides a powerful lens through which to examine our motivations for choosing to pursue a vocation in schools. (For more reflections on Ikigai, see Bethune and Kell, 2020, p.4–5 and for a more detailed exploration of the concept, see Mitsuhashi, 2018.) Figure 1.1 depicts the four key components which

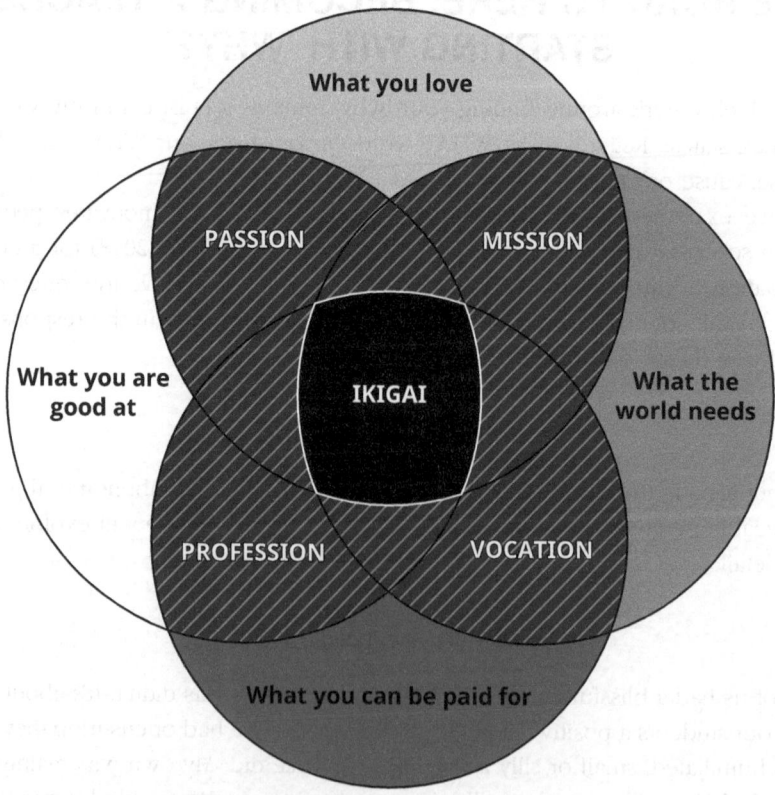

Figure 1.1 You and your Ikigai

contribute to satisfaction and fulfilment; if you're focusing your time and emotional energy on what you love, what the world needs, what you can be paid for and what you know you are good at, you can achieve a sense of mission, vocation, profession and passion – when these four elements come together, you have achieved your Ikigai. Ikigai is closely related to congruence, authenticity, and wellbeing.

Reflection: Your Ikigai

How would you respond to the following questions?

What Gives You Joy?

What elements of your work genuinely give you a deep sense of joy or satisfaction? When do you experience a sense of 'flow' – when you forget yourself, your worries and your concerns and thrive in the moment?

For example, those moments in the classroom when students are fully engaged in a debate or discussion and coming up with brilliant ideas that are 'sparking' off one another. There's an atmosphere of confidence and creativity. (You can read more about finding the joy in teaching in Chapter 7.)

What Does the World Need?

According to your own instinctive sense of social or moral purpose, what does your community or the wider world need to make it a better place?

For example, diverse role models; communities which embrace (rather than merely tolerate) diversity; fair opportunities for all and the courage to call out injustice and inequity.

What Can You be Paid for – and How Much?

We often shy from financial considerations – those working in education are frequently selfless and find it uncomfortable to talk about money, but most of us play a key role as 'breadwinner' at home. This one may take a bit more thought than you'd usually care to give it! You may need to identify your own most pertinent questions but here are some prompts:

How much do you need to earn to keep dependents safe and comfortable?

How much would you like to be earning to experience the lifestyle you (and your loved ones) would like?

What role(s) offer these opportunities?

If you work – or are considering working – part-time, what are the implications of this?

(Continued)

For example, I am relied upon to bring in at least 50% of the household income in order to pay the essential bills – this means I need to be working at least four days a week in a role with some element of responsibility.

What are You Good At?

Another one that isn't often comfortable but it's essential we are aware of our strengths and talents, as if we're not able to channel these towards the people and things that matter, this can result in frustration and restlessness.

What do you *know* you are highly competent at? What have other people praised you for or noticed about you that you are proud of?

For example, I can 'read a room' effectively, picking up on moods and issues quickly and adapt my approach accordingly. I am sensitive to others' needs, emotionally intelligent and able to adapt my communication style to ensure they feel safe, secure and successful.

IF YOU COULD SUMMARISE YOUR IKIGAI IN A SENTENCE, WHAT WOULD IT BE?

Here are some examples.

My Ikigai is to leave the world a better place than I found it by equipping young people with the numeracy skills they need to move into adulthood with a toolkit which makes them savvy, competent and effective.

My Ikigai is to oversee efficient and effective financial management of a school (or schools) to ensure that funds are channelled in line with our ultimate aims – to ensure young people are happy, successful and confident.

My Ikigai is to communicate my passion for Drama to as many young people as I can, because I believe that self-expression is key to future success and happiness.

My Ikigai is to lead a school in which every member of the community feels valued, takes pride in their work, knows they are effective and can ask for help when they need it.

Case Study: Sarina

From Insurance Broker to Teacher

Finding My Ikigai

For nearly two decades, I worked as an insurance broker in the City of London. It was a career I had stumbled into after university, driven largely by the promise of financial stability and a clear trajectory for advancement. On paper, I was doing well – targets met, bonuses earned, promotions ticked off. But over time, I started to feel increasingly hollow. I would find myself sitting at my desk, staring at spreadsheets, wondering what any of it actually meant. I was making rich people richer – but for what?

The tipping point came one rainy Tuesday afternoon. A colleague of mine, recently retired, popped in to say goodbye. As he shook hands around the office, he looked tired, not just physically but in spirit. I remember thinking, *Is that me in 30 years?* I couldn't shake the feeling. That night, I googled *'career change'*, *'meaningful work'*, and eventually stumbled across the Japanese concept of Ikigai – the intersection of what you love, what you're good at, what the world needs, and what you can be paid for. It really struck a chord.

Reflecting on my own experiences, I realised that the moments I felt most alive were when I mentored junior staff or delivered training workshops. I loved breaking down complex topics and seeing that flicker of understanding in someone's eyes. It was a far cry from selling policies, but the seed was planted: maybe teaching was where my Ikigai lay.

I didn't leap straight away. The transition was slow, deliberate, and at times deeply uncomfortable. I enrolled on a part-time PGCE course while working reduced hours. The financial hit was hard – there were days I wondered if I'd made a terrible mistake. I went from a well-respected position in a glass tower to being a 40-something trainee surrounded by fresh-faced grads. Imposter syndrome hit hard.

Teaching itself wasn't the romantic ideal I had imagined, either. My first placement was in a secondary school in an economically deprived area. Behaviour was extremely challenging. Resources were stretched. My colleagues showed little interest in or curiosity about my previous life, let alone tapping into my wisdom as I'd imagined they might. I often went home exhausted, doubting whether I could keep going. But then came those moments – the quiet 'thank you' after a lesson, the pupil who finally grasped a tricky concept, the parent who said I'd made a difference. They were small, fleeting, but they mattered. More than any commission cheque ever had.

I now teach full-time at a further education college, working with students who are often at the margins – those who didn't thrive in mainstream settings, who've faced challenges I can barely comprehend. It's tough. It's emotionally draining. But it's also real. Every day I walk into the classroom knowing I'm doing something that aligns with who I am and what I value.

Finding my Ikigai didn't come with a grand epiphany or a perfect roadmap. It came through trial, doubt, and a lot of self-reflection. I've had to unlearn what success looks like and redefine what fulfilment means. But I wouldn't go back.

Teaching isn't just a job for me now – it's a calling, a craft, and, yes, my Ikigai.

YOU AND YOUR MORAL COMPASS

When I first heard Jill Berry, a former headteacher, consultant, ongoing powerful presence in my life and supporter of thousands of teachers, she used the words, 'hold onto your moral compass'. I'll be honest – I hadn't thought much about values and moral compasses up to that point. I'd thrived up to that point in my career, finding myself in schools where I shared a natural affinity and a shared understanding around agreed ways of working hard (and playing hard!). The motivations behind how I chose to function weren't explicit to me – because I didn't need them to be; they hadn't been openly interrogated or challenged. It was only when I found myself first stumped by an interview question about my values (I paused, stumbled and bumbled through) and then in a school where the culture and expectations *didn't* align with my values, that I was compelled to bring them to the surface and articulate them.

Since then, I've come into contact with numerous school staff in states of confusion or conflict and have found that asking them to explicitly articulate their values is a really powerful exercise.

Let's try it.

Have a look at the list of values below – this is not exhaustive, so feel free to add your own, but I've collated this over several years of working with school staff, based on their varied responses.

Fairness	Risk	Justice
Trust	Inclusion	Order
Growth	Nurture	Understanding
Safety	Generosity	Supportiveness
Dignity	Independence	Openness
Adventure	Reliability	Determination
Success	Integrity	Open-mindedness
Kindness	Love	Authenticity
Humour	Belonging	Playfulness
Public service	Honesty	Courtesy
Humility	Empathy	Insight
Mercy	Stability	Loyalty
Happiness	Compassion	Forgiveness
Autonomy	Candour	Patience
Respect	Resourcefulness	Self-control
Liberty	Simplicity	Credibility
Equity	Creativity	What else?
Excellence	Duty	
Self-knowledge	Curiosity	

Without thinking too hard, make a list of *eight* values which you hold most dear. N.B. These are not (necessarily) your school's stated values or values that you were brought up with, or values that you feel others think you *should* display, but values that you naturally hold as a professional – and values that you hope and expect to see displayed in those around you.

Now, let's map these out on the 'values compass'. There is no *right* or *wrong* way of doing any of these activities – feel free to tweak and adapt, and the values you choose may change or shift over time, depending on your experiences and responses in life and at work.

Your 'true North' is the value that drives you most powerfully from the list of eight; if you could only choose one, what would it be? Your South, East and West are the next three that are most important to you – the values that ground and guide most strongly. For the rest of the points (North East, South East, etc.), you can get 'clever' with it and place values which seem to sit well between your cardinal points, or just put them down where they seem to fit most comfortably (remember, there are no wrong answers!).

In Figure 1.2, you'll see an example of how a completed values compass might look. People often find it useful to physically display their compass above their desk or in another prominent place. You can ask your colleagues how theirs might look…

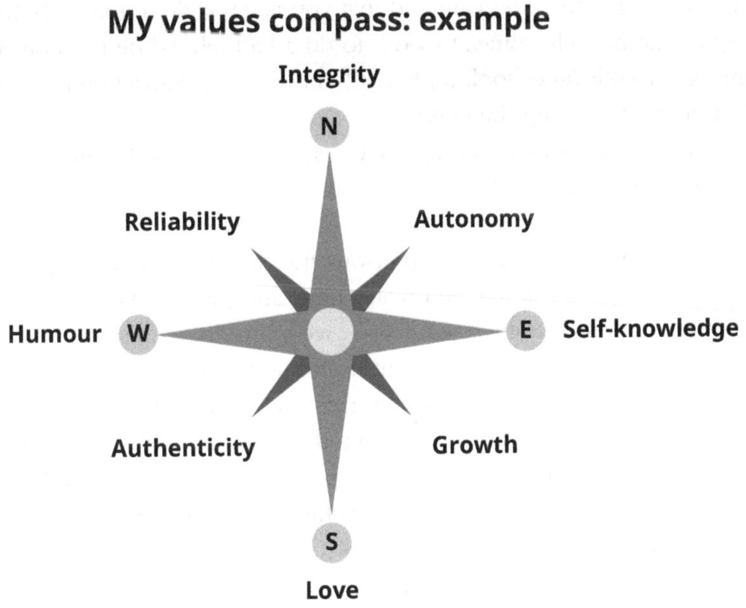

My values compass: example

Figure 1.2 Your values compass

There's loads more you can do with this reflective activity. Here are some ideas.

- Ask yourself (or your team) how a value looks and feels in key elements of your job, e.g. teaching a particular topic, giving difficult feedback, praising a child (or adult!), organising your time and tasks...
- Ask yourself how it feels when this value is overtly challenged or trampled on by others. How does it affect you intellectually, emotionally, even physically? What do you tend to do about it? What *could* you do about it?
- Which of your values sit comfortably together and which are less straightforward bedfellows? For example, how might 'honesty' and 'kindness' or 'excellence' and 'compassion' sit together?

PREPARATION AND FRESH STARTS

Preparing to start a new career or a new role can be a daunting business. The factors behind how daunting it is will be unique to each of us, but a big theme is the sheer volume of unknowns; and most of us struggle with uncertainties and 'what ifs – the gremlins of self-doubt and self-sabotage often revel in climates of uncertainty. They key here is to focus on controlling the controllables.

In the weeks, days and hours preceding a fresh start, worries and sleepless nights are entirely natural. Here are a few tips for taming anxieties in the run-up to the first day and as the first days unfold:

1   Nerves are a sign that you care and that you want to do a good job. In fact, I'd argue that nobody comes to work to do a bad job. I'd be far more worried if one of my colleagues took a blasé attitude of utter conviction they knew it all before even meeting the children.

2   Try not to worry about worrying – that way madness lies! Telling yourself you *shouldn't* be stressed can lead to a vicious spiral. Acknowledge it with trusted people and in secure spaces.

3   If your worry is eating into your precious holiday or weekends and time with loved ones, set aside 'designated worry time' and put it in your diary – this may sound counter-intuitive, but if you give yourself 'permission' to worry between certain times, it helps to put useful boundaries in place.

4   The first day in any new organisation has, in my experience (and I've done it a dozen times or more) *always* been utterly overwhelming and given me total brain fizz. Sift through the thousands of pieces of information you'll receive and zone in on the children you are teaching and their needs, the content of what you need to teach in the first week or so and anything related to safeguarding. The rest can wait, I promise!

5   Prime your team. Who are the key people, within and outside work, who you will be leaning on for sanity, perspective and comfort? It can be useful to ask

them to help keep you accountable, for example for pledges you've made to yourself on working hours and self-care.

6   Remember, you've done one of the hardest bits – you've got the role! A team of experts has put hours into selecting the right person for this role and they've decided it's you. You're already winning! And, whether you're starting your career from scratch or as the Chief Finance Officer, the organisation has a duty of care to you – find out what support is on offer and, firmly but gently, hold the organisation responsible for this (e.g. a weekly line-management meeting to ask questions and check you're on the right track *must* be protected time).

7   Ask all of the questions. I've seen so many talented professionals grow and thrive in this profession, and one of the characteristics that many of the most principled, most effective and most successful have had is that they *asked questions about everything from Day 1*. Don't feel you're being annoying – you're not! Don't make the mistake I did and spend a year on an eight-minute round-trip to the loo because you are too proud to ask where the nearest one is.

8   Assemble a little survival kit for yourself. What it contains will vary from person to person, but snacks and emergency meals are a must, some tissues, a personal memento to remind you that you're a whole human being, sanitary products, a lovely flask and a water bottle are some things you might like to include.

9   Finally, plan something to look forward to! If you're lucky enough to have the means, plan a holiday or short break – October half term in the sunshine is always a winner. Otherwise, just plan a walk with an old friend or a road trip to one of your happy places for a few weeks from now.

FOR LEADERS: INDUCTION OF NEW STAFF

The first minutes, hours, days and weeks in a school will set a blueprint for how effective and happy a staff member is likely to be in your school and will help them understand expectations and cultural norms in your organisation. Getting this bit right is key to healthy retention.

Induction for new staff isn't just about ticking boxes or handing over policies – it's about setting the tone, building relationships, and showing people from the outset that they matter. Here are some thoughts, drawn from experience and the many brilliant colleagues I've learned from over the years.

1   **Start before they arrive:** A welcome message – nothing fancy, just warm and personal – can make all the difference. A quick email, a card in the post, a 'looking forward to working with you' goes a long way in easing those first-day nerves. Send over the timetable, key dates, and the staff handbook ahead of time, so they're not walking in completely blind.

2 **Give them a buddy:** Not just someone who knows the systems, but someone kind, someone who remembers what it's like to be new. A person to chat to in the corridor, to say, 'yes, that room is always freezing' or 'we tend to head to the staffroom around then'.

3 **Make their first day calm and welcoming:** Introduce them to the team, give them time in their classroom, don't overwhelm them with back-to-back meetings. If you're in leadership, pop by and say hello in person. Those small gestures of being seen and valued – especially early on – have a bigger impact than we realise.

4 **Help them feel part of things:** Set up informal chances to meet colleagues over tea or lunch. Show them where the mugs live, how to work the photocopier (or at least who to ask when it breaks). These seemingly tiny things are often the ones that help people settle in.

5 **Don't cram everything into week one:** Stagger the key information across the half term. Give them time to breathe and absorb. Build in check-ins – week 2, week 4, week 6 – where someone asks not just 'have you read the safeguarding policy?' but 'how are you doing?' and means it.

6 **Listen to them:** Ask what's working and what's not. They'll spot things others miss – fresh eyes often do. Be open to their feedback and let them know their voice counts, even while they're still finding their feet.

7 **Celebrate their early wins:** A smile from a tricky student, a lesson that landed, a display put up – notice these things and say so. It boosts confidence and helps create that sense of belonging we all need.

8 **Make sure they know where to go for help:** Whether it's pastoral support, a mental health first aider, or just someone to talk to on a rough day – signpost it clearly and early. And keep reminding them. People don't always ask the first time.

9 **Set a good example when it comes to work–life balance:** If you say wellbeing matters, show it. Don't make late-night emailing the norm. Encourage them to switch off, take their breaks, go home.

10 **And remember, one size doesn't fit all:** A new teacher fresh out of training will need different support to a new head of department. Flex the induction accordingly. Make space for their professional growth, too – let them know from the start that this is a place where people learn and develop.

Ultimately, induction is about humanity. It's about helping people feel safe, seen, and supported in the messy, beautiful business of working in a school. Do it well, and you lay the foundations not just for retention, but for a truly connected team.

For more excellent tips on successful induction, see Cat Priggs' blog, 'We need to talk about... effective staff induction' (2025).

Case Study: Luigi

My Fresh Start

I had been teaching for five years when I decided to move to a new school in a different city. My previous experience had left me unsure about whether teaching was the profession for me. I was excited but also nervous about the change. From the moment I arrived, the school made me feel welcome. My new colleagues were friendly and supportive, and I was assigned a mentor who helped me navigate the school's systems and culture. I appreciated the structured induction programme, which included regular check-ins and opportunities to ask questions. There were plenty of shared resources but I also had plenty of autonomy and was able to be creative in the classroom. I quickly felt part of the team and was able to focus on my teaching. My students responded well to my enthusiasm and innovative teaching methods. By the end of the term, I felt confident and valued in my new role, and I knew I had made the right decision to move.

Case Study: Sara

My Challenging Transition

I had been a teacher for over a decade when I decided to take on a new challenge at a different school. However, my experience was far from positive. From the outset, I felt isolated and unsupported. There was no formal induction programme, and I struggled to find basic information about the school's policies and procedures. My colleagues were busy and seemed indifferent to my presence. I found it difficult to connect with my students, who were used to a different teaching style and kept telling me they missed their previous teacher. I felt overwhelmed by the workload and the lack of support. Despite my best efforts, my confidence began to wane, and I started to question my decision to move. By the end of the term, I was considering leaving the profession altogether.

UNDERSTANDING AND COMMUNICATING HOW WE WORK, COMMUNICATE AND FUNCTION MOST EFFECTIVELY

We each have a responsibility to find professional and clear ways of communicating to our colleagues – and indeed to our students, as is appropriate – and to understand how we function most effectively, and this might require a level of explicit self-examination to which we wouldn't ordinarily give the time and energy. Obviously, whether you're a leader or not, you're not going to please everyone all of the time. You can't create a silent space and a noisy space in the same cramped area to which your team has access; but you could, for example, signpost other quiet areas in the school where team members might like to work when they need to get their heads down, whilst those who like to verbally process their ideas and digress for a chat use the office space. You might also be able to signpost quiet times during the working day, when chatter should be restricted to certain spaces.

We need to be curious and ask the key questions, because we also have a responsibility to understand how our colleagues prefer to function, so we can be considerate of this, within professional boundaries. So, I know that making a last-minute change to a schedule is something that I'd often do without giving it a second thought, seeing myself as responsive and flexible to changing circum-stances – but I also understand that I have colleagues for whom a sudden change of plan would cause serious stress, because they need clarity and meticulous plans in order to feel effective at work.

Here's a really simple and impactful activity that can help. When starting out in a new school year or term, make the time to work through the following prompts with your line manager – make sure they get to share theirs as well, because recip-rocal understanding is key. Obviously, the responses need to be within professional boundaries (nobody is suggesting you ask for an extra day off a week or for some-one to peel your grapes!), but you may be surprised at how powerful this can be. You may want to use this to focus on specific areas of your work (e.g. receiving feedback, organisation of your planning and marking) or keep it more general.

> When working with me, please do…
>
> When working with me, please avoid…
>
> My strengths and value to the team…
>
> I sometimes struggle when…

We go into greater depth on the subject of understanding how we each work, com-municate and function most effectively in Chapter 2.

SETTING YOUR INTENTIONS

You'll be inundated, no doubt, by schemes and plans and targets you're required to follow by your school and your team. But what are *your* professional goals for the term/year ahead? It's worth being really explicit about these and keeping them somewhere prominent. Here's a powerful set of questions you may wish to ask yourself.

Reflection: Goals for Your Stakeholders

Identify your key stakeholders (e.g. students, colleagues, line managers, parents, governors). Set a key milestone (the end of the term or the end of the year). Ask yourself, in relation to you and your role:

What do you want them to be *thinking*?

What do you want them to be *feeling*?

What do you want them to be *saying*?

What do you want them to be *doing*?

You could do this individually or as a team, perhaps with a specific focus – key groups of vulnerable students or a group of parents. It's worth revisiting these at key points to see how far you've come.

CONCLUSION

The path to becoming an educator is as unique as each individual who embarks on it. From the initial spark of inspiration to the daily triumphs and challenges, teaching is a journey of self-discovery and growth. Embracing your authentic self, fostering kindness and compassion, and understanding the diverse qualities that make a great teacher are central themes we've explored. The reflections and case studies shared offer a glimpse into the complexities of teaching and the profound impact educators have on their students' lives. As we move forward, let's hold onto our moral compass, strive for personal growth, and remember that the journey to becoming a brilliant teacher is a deeply personal and rewarding one.

Next, we will delve into the crucial topics of identity, belonging, and relationships, exploring how these elements shape our experiences and interactions within the educational environment.

REFERENCES

Bethune, A. and Kell, E. (2020). *A little guide for teachers: Teacher wellbeing and self-care*. Sage.

Kell, E. (2018). *How to survive in teaching: Without imploding, exploding or walking away*. Bloomsbury.

Mitsuhashi, Y. (2018). *Ikigai*. Kyle Books.

Priggs, C. (2025). 'We need to talk about... effective staff induction'. https://catherinepriggseducation.substack.com/p/17-we-need-to-talk-about-effective

Sinek, S. (2011). *Start with why: How great leaders inspire everyone to take action*. Penguin Books.

2

BELONGING

This chapter explores:

- **Belonging:** Its definition and importance.
- **Maslow's hierarchy:** Belonging's role in self-actualisation.
- **Equity, diversity, inclusion** and how this fosters belonging.
- **Cultural connection** and its importance in the classroom.
- **The components of belonging:** Collective efficacy, compassion, psychological safety, solidarity.
- **Examples:** Practical reflections on belonging in schools.
- **Impact:** Effect on staff wellbeing and performance.

MY STORY

It was an important day at my school of six years, and I'd set off extra early to avoid the traffic. Before settling to the 'to-do' list, I took a wander the long way around the school to my office. I stopped to stroke the guinea pigs in the ASD unit, popped into the caretaker to find out how the battle against the pigeons was going, dropped a crime novel off with the Head of HR (we'd discovered we have similar tastes) and checked in on a group of lark-students whose parents regularly dropped them off early. We discussed the latest exploits of one's pet iguana and compared notes on the latest football scores. I met the deputy head coming in, laden with files, and she stopped to ask about my daughter's latest nocturnal exploits (she too had had a non-sleeping baby). I took the safest route past the Year 10 boys who'd come in early to play football (I'd learned that one the hard way after a ball in the face the year before), smelt the musty-sweet odour of the PE changing rooms and eventually arrived at the office to put the kettle on for the team.

This is what 'feeling part of the furniture' felt like. I was a part of that school and it was a part of me. I belonged. I wasn't, of course, irreplaceable, but that period remains one of the most rewarding and happy of my career.

BELONGING: WHAT IS IT AND WHY DOES IT MATTER?

To feel we belong to a group is a primitive human instinct and, from an evolutionary point of view, is tied to survival – the lone traveller separated from the crowd is far more likely to become prey to mortal danger.

Maslow's hierarchy of needs places 'belonging' – the need for connection and acceptance – at the third tier of the pyramid of human needs. Each of these needs must be fulfilled before 'self-actualisation' can take place; for high performing teams to achieve their purpose, all members of the community feel they can be creative and fulfil their potential.

There's a wealth of research out there on belonging in schools, though much of it focuses predominantly on children (Maslow's hierarchy is no exception). This is of course entirely understandable – they're why we do it. So, taking children as a starting point, let's consider the concept of cultural connection, explored by Kara (2021):

> A culturally connected classroom acknowledges the multiple identities in the room. It is an actively constructed entity designed to create cohesion and understanding. It is a conscious space in which students are made aware of difference and similarity, equity and respect. (p.28)

If we replace the word 'classroom' here with 'school' or 'community' or 'organisation', this concept provides us with a valuable basis on which to begin to consider the concept of belonging in schools. The words 'acknowledge' and 'conscious' are here – for every member of a community to feel a true sense of belonging, they need to feel that their values, their drivers, their skills, their talents and their identities are truly accepted and valued; these are communities in which constant review and reflection take place – nothing is taken for granted.

Case Study: Jane

Rediscovering Belonging Through Inclusion

When I joined my current school, I had just left a setting where inclusion was actively discouraged. I was beginning to doubt whether I still belonged in education. But within a year, everything changed.

Inclusion and belonging are truly valued here – by everyone, from the executive head to support staff. I feel trusted, understood, and able to be myself. Earlier this year, I began seeking an autism diagnosis and was invited to share my experience with students. That level of openness and acceptance has helped me grow both personally and professionally.

Our students thrive because they're genuinely seen and supported, whether in the unit or mainstream classrooms. Inclusion isn't a buzzword here; it's a lived value. It was even recognised during our recent Ofsted inspection, which resulted in our first ever 'Good' rating in 18 years.

I've recently started an NPQSL, and I feel proud to be part of a school and trust that not only talks about values but lives them. I've regained my faith in education – and in myself.

EQUITY, DIVERSITY AND INCLUSION

Equity, diversity and inclusion are an important part of belonging.

Equity

Equity is a commitment to ensuring that everybody has access to the same opportunities. Crucially, it is distinct from the concept of 'equality' because it carefully considers and actively addresses unequal starting points. It is a constant exercise in identifying barriers (intentional or unintentional), including unconscious bias, to ensure systems are fair and just.

To achieve equity, an organisation must be 'constantly and consistently recognising and redistributing power' (Burnette, 2019).

Diversity

Diversity is when 'multiple identities [are] represented in an organisation' (Burnette, 2019). When I read Syed's *Rebel Ideas* (2020), I was struck by his discussion on the power of actively inviting healthy challenge from diverse perspectives: 'Groups that contain diverse views have a huge, often decisive, advantage,' says Syed (p.15). In our organisations, it's essential to ensure that the lived experience and voices of those with protected characteristics are not just acknowledged, but actively celebrated. These characteristics include race, age, disability, gender reassignment, marriage and civil partnership, pregnancy and maternity, race, religion or belief, sex and sexual orientation. Diversity of thought, perspective and approach is also key.

Inclusion

Inclusion is achieved when the 'thoughts, ideas and perspectives of all individuals matter' (Burnette, 2019). It is the active practice of ensuring all individuals in an organisation know they matter – they feel their identity and values are acknowledged, respected, empowered. It's not just about that weasel word 'tolerance' but about actively embracing difference.

Only when each of these three elements – equity, diversity and inclusion – are firmly in place can a sense of true belonging for all members of the community come about. Unlike the other three elements, which are essentially about processes and outcomes, belonging involves an emotional response – one which can often be instinctive and intangible.

To further aid an understanding of how the concept of belonging fits in with the crucial and urgent issues of equity, diversity and inclusion, the work of Krys Burnette is hugely helpful. In her blog, *Belonging: A conversation about equity, diversity and inclusion*, she uses a Venn diagram to illustrate the intersection between equity, diversity and inclusion – all of which are essential to cultures of belonging. The definitions she provides are cited below.

Where only the following are achieved, the results are as follows:

Equity + diversity: Culture assimilation results in disengagement and low retention.

Inclusion + equity: Over saturation of similarity, homogenous culture and simplified points of view.

Diversity + inclusion: The dominant group or ideology is deferred to for decision-making, opportunities and promotions.

Only where all three are present: inclusion, equity and diversity, suggests Burnette, does true belonging become a reality, whereby the organisation engages the full potential of the individuals, innovation thrives and beliefs and values are integrated (Burnette, 2019).

It's important that we are clear about the distinctions between these terms and understand that for a true sense of 'belonging' to exist in an organisation, all components must be subject to careful planning, action and reflection.

KEY COMPONENTS OF BELONGING

In her research, supervisor and coach Dr Rachel Briggs highlights several other factors crucial to a sense of belonging – and overall wellbeing – for school staff:

- Collective efficacy – a shared belief in the combined capacity of the group to create favourable outcomes and environments through its actions.
- Compassion – the collective understanding and empathy towards the emotional and physical wellbeing of others, fostering a supportive and nurturing environment where individuals feel valued and cared for.
- Psychological safety – freedom to make mistakes, to contribute and to challenge without fear of embarrassment or punishment.
- Solidarity – unity from shared values; the collective commitment to support and stand by each other, fostering a sense of unity and mutual respect.

Reflection: Belonging in Your School

Use a blank Venn diagram, like the one in Figure 2.1 to consider what conscious actions your school takes to ensure inclusion, equity, diversity and, ultimately, belonging. What are your next steps to further embed a sense of belonging?

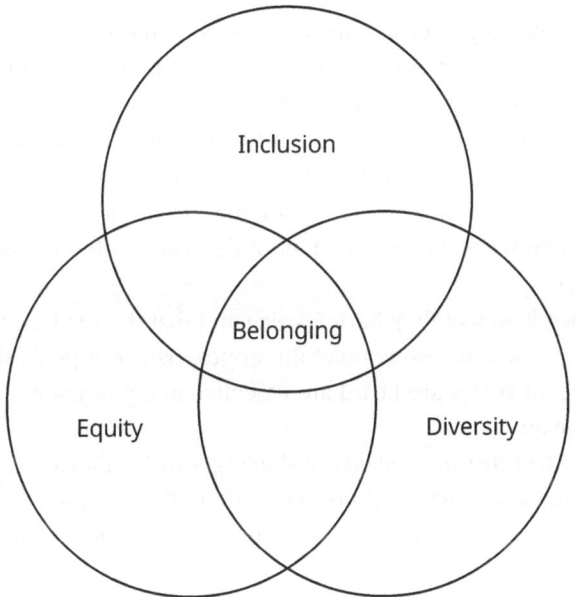

Figure 2.1   Fostering belonging

BELONGING IN PRACTICE

The theory is one thing, but how does this essential and complex concept look in practice?

Teenagers cut to the chase, as ever, and the words from a young person (during a heated discussion about the relative virtues of different chocolate bars), 'Miss, I feel seen! I feel heard!' resound in my head as I write.

The importance of validation and acknowledgement is key. In his Desert Island Discs interview, footballer Ian Wright speaks movingly of the impact his teacher, Mr Pigden, had on him during a traumatic childhood.

'I just felt important...' says a tearful Wright about Mr Pigden. He changed my life just by recognising... I don't know what it was... that I needed more. And he gave it to me.'

In the frequently task-driven and highly performative profession that is working in schools, there is a risk that we can be so busy being busy that we fail to appreciate the importance of those moments of human connection which can do so much to enhance a sense of belonging, acceptance and safety; these are the moments no performance appraisal system can adequately measure or capture, but the ones that are priceless in their worth.

I turned to school staff from a range of settings to ask what 'belonging' means to them. Here are some of the things they said.

- 'It's about coming together in pursuit of a common goal – this is easier said than done; we know where we want to get to but have *very* different ideas about how to get there!' (Deputy head)
- 'For me, it's about authenticity – I need to feel that I can be my real self at work and not fit into a mould that doesn't suit me.' (Teaching assistant)
- 'Listening – really listening – is so important. I try to give people time to be heard but when we're all so rushed all of the time, it's hard!' (Assistant headteacher)
- 'Everyone needs to feel they have a voice and that their voice matters. Obviously, not all at the same time! But appropriate and professional channels to make sure all voices are heard are essential, in my opinion.' (School business manager)
- 'Sometimes I feel that my colleagues don't "get me" – they don't really understand my job or what I do or why I do it. I'm not asking for certificates or a pat on the back, but I'd like to feel more appreciated.' (Family Support Worker)
- 'None of us is perfect – we all have bad days and we all feel vulnerable sometimes. To be able to share our vulnerability in a way which feels right for us is important for belonging.' (Middle Leader)
- 'It's about being aware of the important things – who's having a hard time at home, who's ready for a fresh challenge, whose confidence might need a bit of a boost and ensuring the rest of us do our best to lift one another.' (Headteacher)
- 'Without mutual trust, you can't feel you belong. Feeling that others are a threat, that they are undermining us or think we're rubbish at our jobs totally undermines any sense of belonging and makes us feel uncomfortable and on-edge all the time.' (Pastoral Leader)
- 'Genuine, open curiosity really helps boost belonging. Being open to and receptive of others' stories, experiences and perspectives is so refreshing!' (Reception Teacher)
- 'We're like a family – recently, we had a gas failure, and the canteen couldn't function. Everyone just mucked in, regardless of role, to ensure the children got fed. Nobody expected a reward for it – they did it because we all care about the same things.' (Headteacher)
- 'For me, it's about modelling. For those who are members of a minority, to see people who look and sound and dress a bit like us taking on key influential positions in school leadership makes us think, maybe, one day, that could be me.' (Middle Leader)

It's striking how the themes highlighted by these school staff mirror the research. School culture and norms, 'the way we do things around here' play a key role in determining the extent to which people are likely to feel they belong – or not. School culture is powerfully defined by Peterson and Deal as the 'underground stream of norms, values, beliefs, traditions, and rituals that has built up over time as people work together, solve problems, and confront challenges' (Peterson and Deal, 1998, p.28).

Reflection: Defining 'Belonging'

What does 'belonging' mean to you? Jot it down here. Ask your colleagues what 'belonging' means to them. What do they say?

What's been striking through my own career is that, during the fulfilling and happy periods (which, blessedly, have dominated), I've actually been pretty oblivious to the culture, simply because it has been so closely aligned to my own values and priorities that living it felt as natural as breathing; the sharing of joys and frustrations, the bonding in the pub on a Friday all felt so natural and right that to reflect on them simply wasn't necessary. It was only when I found myself in a context where my values weren't aligned to that of the organisation that I was able to clearly articulate how it felt – and how much it meant – to 'belong'.

MY STORY: AVOIDING EYE CONTACT

It's mid-October and I'm a few weeks into a new middle leadership role. A younger colleague sits down next to me in the staffroom. 'Emma,' he says. 'I've smiled at you and said good morning almost every day – why are you blanking me?' I was totally taken aback and, frankly, horrified by this comment, because I had no idea what he meant. I've always seem myself as warm and approachable (arguably too much so, according to my children, who find my tendency to strike up conversations with strangers excruciating). So what on earth had happened? What had happened was that, until the end of the previous July, I'd worked in a school where I felt fearful almost every day. Where to make eye contact was to risk a reprimand for failing to follow yet another protocol or procedure or dress code that I hadn't registered. Keeping your head down, avoiding human contact (especially with more senior colleagues) had become – without my being remotely conscious of this – a survival technique; a 'natural' way of being. And I'd taken this – again, without realising it – into a new context where others found it cold, rude and, frankly bizarre. It took me several weeks of 'reprogramming' and reminders to return to my gregarious self.

A sense of belonging has a profound impact on staff wellbeing, performance, motivation and confidence. Let's go on to explore some of the factors which contribute to this.

Case Study: Viv

Embracing My Neurodiversity

At 37, I reached out to my GP during a particularly low point. I hadn't taken time off work, but I was struggling with anxiety, low mood, and irritability. I was prescribed antidepressants and referred to a mental health team. There, a specialist suggested I may be autistic, and after pursuing a diagnosis, I was formally identified as being on the autistic spectrum.

I shared this with my school throughout, and the support I received, particularly from a senior leader, was genuinely reassuring. The diagnosis helped me understand myself better. It explained why I'm sometimes seen as 'very direct' or 'a bit intense' by colleagues, and why I occasionally find busy classrooms or corridors overwhelming. But most importantly, it allowed me to embrace how I experience the world.

I'm open with pupils about being neurodivergent, and it often creates a connection with students who share similar experiences. I've had learners approach me privately, grateful to see someone like them in the classroom.

Since becoming a parent, I've worked part-time and continue to do so, even now that my children are older. My diagnosis has helped me make honest choices about what I can manage – balancing teaching, parenting, and being myself. I feel fortunate to work in a school that values me, and where I've been trusted with responsibility even on a part-time basis. I can genuinely say I've found my place.

FACTORS THAT INFLUENCE BELONGING

A multitude of factors influence how belonging feels in a school. Here, I will explore what I feel matters most in terms of belonging and education spaces.

Them and Us: Language Matters

As I write, I reflect on the prevalence of 'us-and-them' language in schools. We often hear it from main scale staff in reference to senior leaders. Dr Rachel Briggs shone a light on this powerfully in a conversation with me in 2022 on the subject of compassionate leadership: 'There are "us" schools, "them and us" schools and "depends on what mood the leader is in" schools.'

We also witness the use of language to underline division in the competition (sometimes healthy, sometimes less so) between teams ('oh, the award always goes to them in PE'), and the divide between teaching and non-teaching staff, where non-teaching staff have been known to be completely overlooked in staff training sessions. On one occasion a member of the finance team described how she was left sitting, bemused, in the hall, for a session on pedagogy entirely irrelevant to her role; on another, a whole office team discovered their names completely missing from the group allocations on the first training day of September. Let's consider the damaging impact of this kind of omission on any sense of belonging.

When describing her challenges in bringing in the new initiative she'd been tasked with as part of her role, it was noteworthy that one middle leader used the first person singular throughout. A colleague in the session picked up on this 'you used "I" throughout – and never "we". That sounds lonely…'.

Reflection: Language Matters

Tune in to the use of language in your school – when do people talk about 'us' and 'them' and does it highlight issues that need to be addressed?

Names Matter!

I don't consider myself a precious person, but I get a visceral reaction when people I don't know particularly well shorten my name to 'Em' – it's akin to someone diving in for a hug when a handshake or simply a wave would be preferable. My own daughters, who have a different surname to me (one with three syllables that is entirely phonetic though not 'western') admitted that almost nobody pronounces it correctly. 'But you correct them, yes?' I asked. 'Of course not! That would be embarrassing!'. I worked with someone known to everyone as Mr G because his name was considered 'too hard' for either children or adults to cope with. This doesn't feel right. Taking the time and energy to get something as simple as somebody's name correct isn't difficult and shows a basic level of respect for their identity. Including a phonetic guide to the pronunciation of people's names in email footers is increasingly common and is a great way of eliminating misunderstandings early on.

Putting People in Boxes: 'Difficult People'

I have sat in several leadership training courses, bright-eyed and wildly enthusiastic with world-changing ambition. Many have had titles including the terms 'managing difficult staff', 'managing tricky characters' or similar. I've never been a fan of the word 'managing' in schools – it either has overtones of just about coping and keeping our heads above water, or it suggests herding, corralling, mastering into submission, with none of the trust and autonomy that are, I continue to argue, central to the joy of working in schools.

Whilst some of these courses had elements of excellence, I'm afraid I learned more about myself and the world from the less-than-helpful elements and the rather fierce debates that followed us into the pub when they ended.

Putting people into categories was a common approach and, to be fair, allowed us to bring scenarios from the workplace efficiently and vividly to life.

It was when we explored he most challenging elements of managing teams that the metaphors, in hindsight, became less helpful. Sounding increasingly like adverts for plumbers, we moved to 'drains' and 'blockers'. The 'drains' roll their eyes the minute a change or new initiative is mentioned, they drag their metaphorical heels, bringing the mood of optimism and determination in the room down.

The 'blockers' throw obstacles in the way of shiny new ideas and we can picture them glaring into space as they drink from *their* mug in *their* corner of the staffroom, quietly plotting the downfall of idealistic new leaders and deliberately, provocatively using the 'wrong' colours to mark students' work.

And of course, it's true that when you're trying to make your mark and earn your stripes, particularly as a new leader, people who apparently won't play ball can be a royal pain in the backside. It can feel like a profound personal attack when the latest piece of research from that conference you went to at the weekend that you *know* will make a positive difference to underachieving boys in Year 10 is received with a barely concealed groan. You can't begin to imagine how many book-looks, lesson drop-ins and learning walks are going to be needed for you to demonstrate 'impact' at your next performance appraisal meeting.

'We've told them to do it! Why don't they just do it?' said a frustrated SLT member leading on teaching and learning to me with pure exasperation.

I always considered myself pretty well-behaved and compliant until I found myself in a couple of schools where I seemed to constantly and inadvertently find myself 'in trouble'; for making decisions without appropriate consultation, for wearing a sparkly top ('you're a member of SLT, you're not going clubbing'), for questioning an educational approach on social media that we'd recently introduced in our school... Arguably, I was in the wrong on each occasion and should have paid more attention to expectations, but it does lead me to reflect on how schools either embrace or resist the 'mavericks' in their communities.

I find myself regularly returning to Matthew Syed's *Rebel Ideas*, in which the power of diverse ways of thinking – the potential for human performance that exists when we actively seek out challenge – is explored, and the danger of surrounding ourselves with people who look and act just like us is highlighted.

> Think how comforting it is to be surrounded by people who think in the same way, who mirror our perspectives, who confirm our prejudices. It makes us feel smarter. It validates our world view [...] These dangers are as ancient as mankind itself. (Syed, 2020, p.49)

Beware of Sparkling Boxes Too

Conversely, many schools, whether implicitly or explicitly, have their 'rising stars'; their 'safe pairs of hands'; their 'solid effort' staff. By categorising in this way, are we exerting unnecessary pressures, creating unnecessary divides and risking that our safe pairs of hands eventually burn out because everybody starts asking them to do everything all of the time?

The instinct to categorise people is entirely natural and helps us make sense of the world, but how helpful is it, really, to put people into homogenous clumps? Every group of human beings represents a range of motivations, approaches and challenges that is infinitely complex, and showing curiosity in order to gain understanding of what makes them tick is key.

The Dangers of Assumption

Some time ago, in a role which was otherwise deeply rewarding and fulfilling, I spent years (literally) convinced a colleague loathed me and saw me as deeply incompetent. Granted, this was to an extent fuelled by other colleagues (beware the 'watch out for her/him', which though ostensibly helpful, very rarely is!). It was only when I received what remains one of the sagest pieces of advice from an excellent line manager that I was able to break the cycle of resentment and defensiveness. The four words 'ask her for advice' changed everything. I was working on a specific area for a leadership course I was doing and she really was an expert in this area, one to which I'd had very little exposure. I asked her advice and she was extraordinarily helpful – I learned a great deal from her. I didn't just learn more about the specific focus of the project, but about the dangers of the assumptions I had made. I was impetuous and impulsive (still relatively young and new to the career, but quite ambitious). I was struck by sudden ideas – often way outside my remit and I would frequently find myself way outside my lane, embroiled in tasks well outside my job description, like canteen food and the state of the TAs' office… I was also frequently utterly exhausted and (oh, hindsight), often not doing my actual job as well as I could have done. She didn't beat around the bush with her challenges and feedback and got to the point. By gradually building a bridge between us, I probably learned more than I ever would have from someone who approached the world like me.

The theme of assumptions was also prevalent in accounts from other school staff in the context of a sense of belonging – or lack thereof. Here in the UK, our system is frequently fraught with hyper-accountability and a deficit 'not good enough' approach, and the impact of this on human behaviour can often be to feel an overwhelming need to prove ourselves. This instinct can lead us to divisions and the perception of others (who arguably share the same ultimate aims we do; to improve the lives and futures of young people). We are also often rushed and time-poor, so it's 'easier' to act on our gut and make snap-judgements about others, allowing our perceptions to last for (in some cases) years. We can be quick to label others as flaky, rude, cold or power-hungry based on minimal evidence. To be on the receiving end of such a label can leave colleagues feeling ostracised and isolated and ultimately, a member of staff who feels this way is unlikely to stick around for long – this has the potential to compound the existing staff retention crisis…

Let's build on the 'knowing me, knowing you' reflection activity from Chapter 1. Understanding and communicating how we work, communicate and function most effectively The below is based on a task I often take into schools – one that has helped to open up dialogue and challenge such damaging assumptions. Have a look at the headings below. Consider how you *prefer* to communicate/respond/organise yourself in each of the following areas. N.B. This doesn't mean you *can't* be flexible but if there are too many areas where you're forced (by cultural norms, institutional expectation or simple oversight) to react in ways which fall outside your preferred ones, this can lead to high levels of strain and ultimately to stress levels hitting breaking point.

Physical Spaces

At the time of writing, I have had no fewer than three conversations in which people have eventually found themselves discussing physical resources and desk spaces. These colleagues were feeling discombobulated but couldn't quite put their finger on why. In the case of a client who'd recently been diagnosed with ADHD, and was acutely aware of her susceptibility to sensory overload, it transpired that the department was quite a mess and she struggled to find a clear, quiet space in which to do her planning and marking. In another, a few weeks into a new role, the person did not yet have a desk assigned to them at all (unlike their colleagues) and were somewhat sheepishly 'parking' at different desks and hoping they wouldn't be shouted at. In both cases, there were clear next steps (if not straightforward ones!) to carve out the space they needed.

Reflection: Physical Spaces

What kind of physical space do you need to think/reflect/plan most effectively? Do you have it? If not, how could you create it or seek it out?

Praise and Acknowledgement

To feel recognised for our expertise and impact is a common need but one that varies hugely in it its nature from one individual to another. Whilst some colleagues may respond to public recognition of their efforts, others may prefer a quiet word of thanks – for others still, simply knowing their actions have helped a young person or the organisation is enough. As a phenomenon, appreciation is often most striking in its absence – this links back to failing to recognise the contributions of key groups and key individuals appropriately and fairly in the school. Making sure there are a range of mechanisms for expressing acknowledgement is key – this might sound complex, but in fact, my research and experience says the quiet 'thank you' or the handwritten card can have more impact than a shout-out board or certificate.

Reflection: Acknowledgement

How do you prefer to be acknowledged for the work you do? What about your colleagues? Do they differ or are they similar?

Relationships at Work

Through my career, I've known colleagues meet their future spouse and lifelong friends through work. Depending on the demands and realities of our lives at any given time, each of us has different needs from our relationships with colleagues. Many will work hard and play hard together, with frequent contact beyond work, and this will give them deep fulfilment. For others, their job may simply need to be just that – their responsibilities beyond work may take up their emotional attention and energy and they may prefer their relationships at work to be purely professional. I have one colleague who's recently returned to work after a long and serious illness. 'I don't want to be rude,' she said, 'and I really appreciate it that people care, but I just want to get my head down and get on with the work. I don't want fuss'.

Whether intimate or distant, as long as professional standards are being met, all approaches to relationships at work should be accepted for a sense of belonging to be strong in the workplace. Whilst a staff party might be the highlight of one staff member's end of term, for another, just getting home to loved ones might be a bigger priority.

We'll build more on the power of relationships in the following chapter.

Reflection: Relationships at Work

What do you need from your relationships at work? What about those around you?

Challenging Assumptions

When challenging assumptions, you may also wish to consider that we each take different approaches to the following – how does your workplace cater to different preferences?

- Routines and time-management.
- Receiving feedback.
- Challenging conversations.

- Emails, paperwork, data.
- Technology.
- Noise and noise levels.
- Stressors and triggers.
- Giving and receiving instructions/guidance.
- Meetings.

FOR LEADERS: CONTRACTING CONVERSATIONS

Build in structured time (e.g. in your expectations of line-management meetings) for these kinds of 'contracting' conversations at all levels and by all leaders and managers. Revisit them regularly, particularly during times of professional or personal transition. Model this kind of explicit communication – 'you know I'm the kind of person who trusts you to get on with it but appreciates you checking in every week or so to update me on your progress'; 'you know I'm not someone who expresses their emotions easily but please rest assured that I appreciate your efforts.'

BELONGING AND BUBBLES: FINDING A BALANCE

There is one caveat – or note of caution – that I would argue comes with advocating a sense of belonging in a school, and it's around the danger of becoming too firmly ensconced in a single bubble. Looking outwards is essential, be it through wider reading, educational conferences, or building a network of people in similar roles in other organisations. Whilst high staff retention is often a positive thing, a healthy turnover of staff to ensure fresh faces and fresh perspectives is also important. The danger with organisations where 'nobody leaves' is that challenge to the status quo is minimised and this, as we have discussed, can be stifling. We can 'belong' in more than one professional community, and I'd advocate seeking out others for healthy debate, research and support.

THE IMPACT OF A LACK OF BELONGING

The sense that we don't belong in a school may be telling us something important and powerful. I've said before and will say again that my experiences in a variety of different schools have differed so widely that it's sometimes felt like working in a completely different profession – and sometimes, the gut sense that we don't belong can be a healthy and important impetus to move on and find a new context to work in.

It's more likely, however, that lack of attention to nurturing a sense of belonging (alongside workload and stress) leads teachers early in their careers to give up on the profession – we know that 43,522 teachers left the profession in the UK in 2023 (Booth, 2024).

Within schools, a lack of belonging can lead to conflict, ostracism of individuals and groups and, most crucially, the diversion of emotional attention and energy, which should be invested in our young people.

Case Study: Pascale

Navigating the Motherhood Penalty in Teaching

I trained to be a teacher at 26 and, in the three years before having my first child, my career was progressing well. I was told I was ready for a leadership role, but becoming pregnant changed everything. I worked in a Catholic school and was asked to hide the fact that I wasn't married, which left me feeling isolated and unsupported.

After maternity leave, I was fortunate to return part-time as requested, but I constantly felt guilty – as if I had to prove myself by doing a full-time job in part-time hours. Things eventually came to a head when I questioned the senior leadership's response to me leaving work for my child's emergency GP appointment. I was threatened with disciplinary action and felt I had no choice but to leave.

I turned to supply teaching for what I thought would be a year but ended up staying longer. A long-term supply post at the same school allowed me to rebuild my confidence and rediscover a sense of balance, though even then, I was once called into the office for leaving at 4 pm.

This experience sparked my focus on mental health and wellbeing. I became a Mental Health and Wellbeing Lead, where I could address the lack of understanding and proper systems in place. Eventually, I set up my own organisation to continue this work. In 2022, I returned to full-time teaching for the first time in ten years. While I often feel I should be further ahead career-wise, I recognise the strength and insight I've gained through this journey.

Case Study: Chantelle's 'Resting Bitch Face'

During the lockdown period, I completed the NASENCo award [a UK award for Special Needs and Disabilities Co-Ordinators in school]; I was keen to develop and share my expertise with staff whilst simultaneously line-managing a team of LSAs and overseeing SEND across the academy. When invited to speak about

(Continued)

career development, I sat outside the Principal's office waiting to be called in as she was otherwise engaged. The meeting, not to my surprise, did not go as anticipated but instead homed in on how I should 'slow down' and that I was 'ambitious and exactly where I needed to be in my career as deputy SENDCo'. It was at this point that this compounded what I believed at the time to be true: progression doesn't happen for people like me... for people that look like me... for Black women. This opened my eyes to ways in which the system continues to dampen the zeal and passion of diverse members under the guise of kindness and empathy. I felt as though I could not make a mistake as I would be con-demned. The comment that I had a 'resting bitch face' confirmed that even my innocent (I shouldn't even have to use the word) mannerisms and body language are policed and criticised. At a later point, I was told I was 'being watched' and that my facial expressions had improved – make of that what you will. Fast for-ward three years, I'm now leading on anti-racism as no educator should be subjected to unfair treatment. This was not an isolated incident and it gave me the ammunition to shift the narrative around what it means to be a Black female leader and educator.

BENEFITS OF BELONGING

If schools can foster a healthy sense of belonging, this is likely to have a powerful impact. If we feel 'part of' an organisation and share in its values, we are more likely to put in discretionary effort – to go above and beyond the job description, enrich-ing our students' experiences within and beyond the building. Our commitment is likely to be greater; we arrive home on a Friday, almost certainly exhausted, but with a sense of satisfaction and self-efficacy – we, as a community, have done a great job and I, as an individual, have played a crucial role in this. We're likely to feel trusted and more able to innovate and reflect, resulting in quality provision for our young people. In short, we're likely to feel happier, and if we feel happier, we're more likely to stick around.

CONCLUSION

The concept of belonging is fundamental to human experience and plays a crucial role in our wellbeing and performance at work. This chapter has explored the vari-ous dimensions of belonging, including its definition, importance, and the factors that contribute to it. From Maslow's hierarchy of needs, to practical reflections on belonging in schools, we have seen how belonging impacts staff wellbeing and per-formance. By fostering equity, diversity, and inclusion, we can create environments where everyone feels valued and connected. Ultimately, a strong sense of belonging leads to happier, more motivated, and more effective teams, benefiting both individuals and the wider community.

REFERENCES

Booth, S. (2024). 'Teaching workforce grows by just 259 as recruitment stalls'. *Schools Week*, 6 June. https://schoolsweek.co.uk/teaching-workforce-grows-by-just-259-as-recruitment-stalls

Burnette, K. (2019). *Belonging: A conversation about equity, diversity and inclusion.* www.krysburnette.com/blog/belonging-a-conversation-about-equity-diversity-amp-inclusion

Garratt, J. (2024). 'The Johari window'. *Psych Safety*, 16 August. https://psychsafety.com/the-johari-window

Kara, B. (2021). *A little guide for teachers: Diversity in schools.* Sage.

Peterson, K. D. and Deal, T. E. (1998). 'How leaders influence the culture of schools'. *Educational Leadership, 56*(1), 28–30.

Syed, M. (2020). *Rebel ideas: The power of diverse thinking.* John Murray.

Wright, I. and Laverne, L. (2020). *Desert Island Discs* [radio broadcast], 16 February. www.bbc.co.uk/sounds/play/m000fdxw

3

RELATIONSHIPS

RELATIONSHIPS WITH OUR STUDENTS

This chapter explores:

- **Relationships** in schools and the link with **engagement**, **behaviour**, and **academic outcomes**.
- **Supportive relationships** between teachers and colleagues.
- **Managing difficult relationships** and reflecting on how we are perceived.
- Practical tips for building **strong relationships**.
- Strategies for reframing **tricky relationships**.

In this chapter, we examine the importance of relationships in schools. As I write, I've recently returned from a short, refreshing seaside break with a friend I taught with in the earliest days – a friendship forged over intense school trips (I still dream of counting children in busy European city centres – or worse, of forgetting to count them on ferries). We enjoyed Friday 4 pm pints and plentiful black humour – turns out we can still tap into the silly giggles and belly laughs. I am also preparing to attend the wedding of a student I taught 21 years ago.

MY STORY: MICHEL

I still remember Michel. Couldn't sit still. Constantly tapping, drumming, humming. Could frequently be found crawling under desks. He was described by staff as 'a handful', 'distracting', 'annoying'. In trouble inside school and out. His name seemed to be permanently under the 'sad face' on the board, and he was a permanent resident in detentions. But underneath it all, he was smart, funny and wanted to do well. He just didn't fit the narrow mould. These days, I suspect he might have been diagnosed with ADHD. I tried to keep showing up, even when he pressed my buttons. I listened, challenged when I had to, and laughed with him whenever I could. Twenty years later, I bumped into him in the supermarket of all places.

Shirt and tie, trolley full of groceries, smile wide. He told me he was working as a project manager for a construction firm, had a mortgage and a family, and said, 'You were the first teacher who didn't give up on me. I never forgot that.' That moment – those words – are why we do what we do.

RELATIONSHIPS WITH OUR STUDENTS

Building positive relationships with young people isn't just important – it's essential, and though this can be time-consuming, it's worth putting in the effort and reminding ourselves regularly that they are still growing and forming – fresh starts (every lesson, every day, every week) are key. Children and adolescents are hard-wired to test boundaries, not out of malice, but as part of how they learn, grow, and figure out the world around them (Pianta et al., 2012). They are exquisitely attuned to authenticity; they know, almost instinctively, whether or not you care (Roorda et al., 2011). And once they sense that you do – once they feel seen and respected – that is when your impact starts to change lives. They care less about perfection and more about whether you're real: whether you listen, whether you have stories, whether you treat them as people, not projects or coloured blobs on a spreadsheet. In these relationships lie the power to influence, to guide, to inspire; and, crucially, to be inspired in return. Positive student–teacher relationships are also consistently linked in the research with increased engagement, better behaviour, and improved academic outcomes (Cornelius-White, 2007; Hughes, 2011).

TOP TIPS FOR BUILDING STRONG RELATIONSHIPS WITH YOUNG PEOPLE:

- **Be consistent but responsive**: Boundaries matter but warmth, and being attuned to their responses matter just as much.
- **Be unapologetically human**: Admit mistakes, laugh at yourself, share a bit of who you are.
- **Notice the little things**: The new haircut, the quieter mood, the effort made.
- **Hold high expectations:** Show you believe in them. Praise them when they are successful.
- **Don't take it personally**: The eye-rolls, the silences, the tests are rarely about you.
- **Show up again and again**: Trust is built on consistency, in the 'being there', even when it's hard.

THE IMPORTANCE OF HEALTHY COLLEGIAL RELATIONSHIPS

Supportive relationships between teachers and their colleagues – whether mentors, line managers, or peers – are fundamental to staff wellbeing, retention, and professional growth. When teachers feel trusted, respected, and genuinely supported, they are more likely to thrive, collaborate effectively, and remain committed to their roles, even during challenging times. Positive professional relationships not only offer a protective factor against stress but also foster a sense of belonging and shared purpose within schools (Day and Gu, 2010; Collie et al., 2012). Trusting, emotionally intelligent leadership and mentoring relationships are particularly powerful in shaping a healthy school culture and sustaining teachers over time (Tschannen-Moran, 2009). You may wish to refer back to Chapter 2 for tips on building mutual understanding.

THE COLLEAGUES WHO RAISE AND INSPIRE US

'What's the best thing about this job? The people. What's the hardest thing about this job? The people...' I remember a deputy head I worked with once sharing this truism and it continues to resonate.

Schools are messy, beautiful, intricate microcosms of society, in which we have the opportunity to see humanity at its most transformational and most noble – and, at times, at its darkest, most defensive and most destructive.

Few education professionals enter the profession without the expectation that the needs and requirements of young people are likely to be complex and sometimes difficult. However, it is the relationships with other adults that I've found, through my research and experience, to be most critical in determining success, self-efficacy and wellbeing in our professional roles.

THE COLLEAGUES WHO LIFT US

Take a moment to consider your colleagues – imagine them sitting in a circle around you. Make sure you include them all – the caretaker who greets you in the morning, the lunchtime supervisor who always wears beautiful scarves, the trainee teacher who brought in fresh ideas and humility, the business manager who's a mine of expertise. Let's challenge those hierarchies for a moment Whilst I hope you have a line manager who inspires and supports, remember that these can come from all sorts of directions and in all sorts of forms – supportive colleagues might also come from beyond your school building, from within your trust, educational networks, your local authority…

Reflection: Who Lifts You?

Take a moment to consider the following questions and jot down your responses; you might want to pick the questions that are most powerful for you or formulate your own.

Who Has the Ability to…

Make you laugh when you're down?

Make you feel safe when life or work feel precarious?

Challenges you in a helpful way?

Has expertise in areas where you need a bit of help?

INSPIRATIONS

Now let's look at the bigger picture. Look back over your career – over your life as a whole – and consider for a moment those people who shaped and moulded you with positive modelling and human connection. I count the following amongst my own inspirations.

My formidable Year 6 primary school teacher, Mrs Stoneley, whose high expectations and steadfast consistency always inspired me to be better – to do better. Fred, my unflappable, quiet, measured, kind line manger, who would talk me down from the top of trees of sheer panic and certain failure, and say a line I continue to use: 'you are not alone'. Yvonne, who I was convinced loathed me for many years, so different were we, and from whom I suddenly realised I had so much to learn. John, the headteacher who held us to account for insisting students took their coats off in lessons, who terrified me as I sometimes rolled my eyes, and from whom I learned so much about sweating the small stuff… The student, with whom I'd frequently wrangled over his horizontally laid-back attitude and refusal to pull his finger out, who managed to diffuse an alarming and ongoing feud between two groups of girls with the words 'will this matter in five years time?'

I asked education professionals this question. The responses were poignant and powerful and highlight some powerful themes, from the power of good leaders to inspire and heal to the vital importance of believing in people. Here are a few of them:

My first head of department really moulded me – thanks to her, I feel passionate about my subject and confident in my knowledge. Her classroom management was inspiring, and now I can get a room full of teenagers quiet just with a facial expression.

Words from 'a master of kindness and mentor to all': 'Work harder out of the classroom if things are not working. See the child, notice the child, be kind and always forgive.' I now have 33 years in the profession and this is still the best advice.

My headteacher gave me back my confidence and believed in me more than any other leader. He was a very genuine and thoughtful headteacher, with the ability to push me into things that I would not have otherwise done (and sometimes didn't want to do!!).

The best Headmistress I ever worked for. I came to her school after a traumatic experience in the state sector where staff were bullied and intimidated. She showed absolute faith in me from day one and knew all the staff including their families from ground staff to SLT. She gave me back my confidence. She remains a fantastic role model and friend who supported me long after she left the school.

In a performance management review just over a year ago, my line manager went through all of the formalities and then at the point when the meeting should have finished, he put away his laptop and asked me about my aspirations. I had had a rubbish year previously and he knew it, so I was nervous sharing that I wanted to become an AHT. He didn't pause. He absolutely backed me to do it. A couple of months later, he rang me and asked me to take a role at one of our new schools. I asked for leadership, which was ballsy, but he agreed and gave me the opportunity.

Since starting in the toughest school environment I have ever worked in, he has consistently had my back. He is available on the phone, he will listen to any dilemma, provides professional challenge and a rigorous sounding board. He constantly reminds me that I can do it even when I am full of self-doubt. I have learned so much this last term: about myself as a leader and practitioner, about school improvement and about who I want to be as a leader. No one had ever had faith in me before. This person has made so much difference and I'm not sure they are even aware.

A few simple words – a gesture of faith, support or challenge – become a talisman, a refrain. They have a lasting impact and become a part of our values, our professional identity. They often represent what we needed to hear – or needed to feel – even if we didn't realise it at the time, and sometimes when they weren't necessarily what we wanted to hear.

WHEN RELATIONSHIPS WITH COLLEAGUES ARE STRAINED

And, as I write, I reflect on my own periods of struggle – and on hundreds of conversations with those who've struggled, and I would venture that, on the whole, people don't leave schools because of children's behaviour or poor systems and procedures, but because of strained relationships with colleagues.

LEARNING FROM THE TRICKY RELATIONSHIPS

I've learned never to underestimate the damage a toxic relationship can do to a person's confidence, sense of self-worth and likelihood of remaining happily in the profession. If you're convinced someone 'has it in' for you, thinks little of your skills, talents or experience, has put you in a negative box or is actively bullying you, it really can bring you down in significant and career-changing ways – I see it all the time in coaching. And sometimes it does end up being a case of simply getting out and finding a new context to work in – especially if that person has significant influence over you. But there can also be ways of reframing the difficult relationship to help you reach a state, at worst of professional indifference to that person or people or, at best, to help you build some understanding with them.

TIPS FOR REFRAMING TRICKY RELATIONSHIPS

- **Zip up your invisible space suit**. This powerful image was shared with me by a usually calm colleague, after we'd been openly criticised in front of our colleagues and we were both feeling very stung. Imagine zipping up a protective suit – one that keeps in *your* positive energy any keeps out any potential negativity likely to drain you. This helps you protect your emotional space.
- **Boundaries**. I make no apology for returning to these time and time again – healthy boundaries are key. You do not have to respond to every email immediately, stay late every night, or absorb the moods of others. It's perfectly fine to say, 'I'm not able to take that on right now,' or 'Let's pick this up tomorrow.' If you model respecting your own limits, others are likely to follow suit.
- **Reframing** (without necessarily excusing) is powerful. Instead of stewing over 'What is their problem?' or 'Why on earth would anyone behave like that?', try 'What might be going on for them?' It's not about excusing bad behaviour – it's

about freeing *you* from carrying the weight of it. People behave in less-than-ideal ways for all sorts of reasons. Most of the time, it's not about you.

- **Ration your emotional energy**. Are you losing sleep over someone else's bad day? Replaying conversations in your head? Be honest: is this draining more from you than it's giving? Are they likely to be spending half as much energy on this issue? Your energy is precious. Spend it wisely.
- **Keep records**. In some cases, it helps to document things. Not in a dramatic, 'I'm taking this to HR' kind of way (unless you need to), but calmly and professionally. Dates, facts, emails. Keep a clear record. It's a way of protecting yourself if things escalate – and it helps you feel more in control.
- **Seek support, not gossip**. Venting feels good in the moment, but it rarely solves much. Talk to someone you trust. Someone who will listen, help you reflect, and remind you of who you are. You deserve that.

Remember: you don't have to be everyone's best friend; this is a professional environment, not a social club. You don't have to fix anyone. But you do deserve to feel safe, respected, and valued in your workplace.

Case Study: Liam

Finding My Place in the Staffroom

I joined a large secondary school in the Midlands as an English teacher. It was my third year in teaching, and I brought energy, creativity, and a passion for inclusive education. However, from the very beginning, I struggled to connect with my colleagues.

The staffroom felt cliquey, with many staff having long-established social and professional circles. While interactions were polite, they were brief, and I often found myself eating lunch alone or working through breaks. Invitations to team socials seemed to pass me by, and informal discussions rarely included me.

This lack of connection began to affect my confidence. I found it hard to ask for help or share challenges, fearing I would be seen as an outsider. Though my teaching remained strong, the isolation took its toll on my wellbeing.

After a term of feeling adrift, I decided to take small but intentional steps to shift the dynamic. I started by attending every departmental meeting with questions prepared, contributing positively, and offering to share resources. I volunteered to help organise a World Book Day event, working closely with a few colleagues in the process. Gradually, I found allies – teachers who were friendly, open, and eager to collaborate.

By the end of the academic year, I felt much more connected. I wasn't part of every group, but I had found my own network of supportive colleagues. More importantly, I realised that professional respect and relationships often take time to build, and that consistent presence and kindness go a long way.

FOR LEADERS: MANAGING RELATIONSHIPS BETWEEN STAFF

Let's be real – your staff team is the heart of your school. You can have the best policies, the flashiest improvement plans, the shiniest Ofsted report... but if the relationships between adults in your building are broken, none of it works.

So, as a leader, how do you *actively* foster a culture where relationships thrive? And what do you do when the atmosphere starts to turn?

1 **Start with modelling:** You set the tone. The way you talk to people – at briefings, in corridors, when you're under pressure – *matters*. Are you calm, consistent, and kind? Do you show people that you value them, even when you're busy? Small things – greetings, thank yous, remembering names – add up. This isn't about being 'nice' for the sake of it; it's about modelling the respect you want everyone to show each other.

2 **Make relational culture visible:** Talk about it. Prioritise it. Don't just focus on behaviour between students; what about behaviour between staff? Make kindness and professionalism a shared expectation, not a soft add-on. Include it in policies, CPD, staff meetings. Make it part of how your team does business.

3 **Nip negativity early:** If you hear gossip, passive aggression, or undermining behaviour – don't ignore it. You don't need to launch a full-scale investigation, but do have the quiet conversation. 'I noticed that comment. Can we talk about how that landed?' You're not policing personalities; you're safeguarding your culture.

4 **Listen to – and believe – your team:** Sometimes, the 'difficult colleague' is actually a symptom of a wider issue. Ask questions. What's really going on? Is someone unsupported? Burnt out? Feeling invisible? You don't need to have all the answers, but being genuinely curious, and not immediately defensive, can change the whole dynamic.

5 **Use restorative approaches where you can:** If there's a breakdown between staff members, try a facilitated conversation. Give people a safe space to be heard. It won't always lead to perfect harmony, but it can shift things from resentment to resolution. Don't assume time will heal things – it usually doesn't.

6 **Celebrate healthy relationships:** Name and notice collaboration, kindness, and mutual support. Highlight great team moments – shared wins, peer support, acts of generosity. What you praise gets repeated.

7 **Create safe routes for concerns:** Make sure staff know how to raise concerns about unprofessional or bullying behaviour, and that they'll be taken seriously. Psychological safety means people feel confident they'll be heard, without retaliation or being labelled 'difficult'.

8 **Look after your own wellbeing, too:** Supporting staff through conflict can be draining. You're not a therapist. Get supervision if you need it. Talk to trusted colleagues. Protect your own energy so you can lead with clarity and compassion.

9 **And finally, be brave:** Sometimes, tough decisions have to be made. If someone is repeatedly damaging team morale and not responding to feedback or support, it's your job to act. Avoiding it helps no one; not the rest of the team, not the culture, and ultimately, not the person themselves.

Great staff relationships don't happen by accident. They need nurturing, protecting, and prioritising. But when they're strong, everything else flows more easily – from teaching and learning to whole-school morale.

A STEP-BY-STEP GUIDE TO THE WINDOW TO REFLECT, CONNECT AND GROW

Working in education means being *on* – a lot. You're managing students, staff, systems, and yourself, all before managing a couple of gulps of your first cup of coffee. But how often do you stop and ask: 'How do I come across? What do others see in me that I might be missing?'

The Johari window (Luft and Ingham, 1955) is a simple but powerful tool to help you explore self-awareness and deepen relationships.

Reflection: Johari Window

You'll need: ten minutes, some headspace, and Figure 3.1 (the window), and the lists of positive adjectives and challenging adjectives below.

Step 1: Get to Know the Window

1 **Open area:** Traits you know about yourself *and* that others see too.
2 **Blind spot:** Traits others see in you, but that you're not fully aware of.
3 **Hidden area:** Traits you know but keep to yourself.
4 **Unknown area:** Traits or behaviours that neither you nor others have spotted yet.

The goal? To expand your *open area*, where self-awareness, trust, and healthy relationships live.

(Continued)

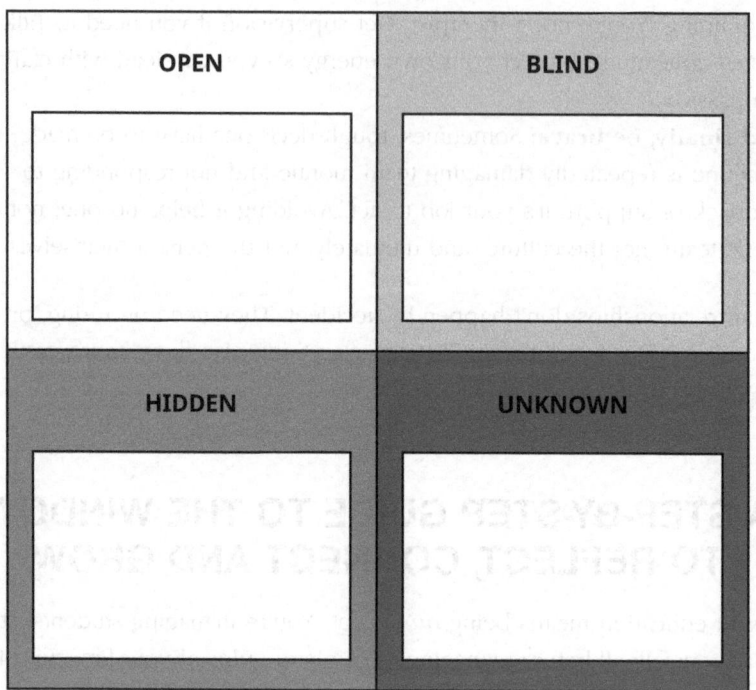

Figure 3.1 Johari Window

Step 2: Choose Your Positive Traits

Look at the list below and choose or note down five–six words you think describe you in your current role.

Adaptable	Diligent	Honest
Adventurous	Diplomatic	Idealistic
Affectionate	Disciplined	Imaginative
Ambitious	Eager	Insightful
Assertive	Efficient	Intellectual
Balanced	Empathetic	Kind
Calm	Energetic	Loyal
Charismatic	Fair-minded	Mature
Cheerful	Flexible	Observant
Compassionate	Friendly	Optimistic
Considerate	Generous	Organised
Courageous	Genuine	Outgoing
Creative	Gracious	Passionate
Decisive	Hardworking	Patient
Dependable	Helpful	Peaceful

Pleasant	Responsible	Unassuming
Polite	Self-reliant	Unbiased
Practical	Sensitive	Understanding
Proactive	Sincere	Versatile
Punctual	Sociable	Vivacious
Receptive	Tactful	Warm
Reliable	Thoughtful	Witty
Resourceful	Tolerant	
Respectful	Trustworthy	

These are the qualities you see in yourself – own them. There's no need for false modesty.

Step 3: Gather Feedback (If You're Feeling Brave)

Ask one or two trusted colleagues to do the same – pick five–six traits from the above list that describe *you*, from their perspective.
   Then compare:

- Traits that match = your *open area*.
- Traits you didn't pick = your *blind spot*.

These surprises can be powerful – someone might see you as *calm under pressure* even when you feel anything but.

Step 4: Reflect on the Hidden Area

Ask yourself: which of these traits do *you* know you have, but rarely let others see?
   Maybe you're *playful*, but worried it won't seem professional. Or *empathetic*, but hide it behind humour or busy-ness.

- Why do I keep this side hidden?
- Would showing a little more of it help build trust?
- What's the cost of keeping it invisible?

Step 5: Explore the Negative Adjectives

Now, deep breath – it's time to look at the list of negative adjectives below; the less comfortable list.

Aloof	Blunt	Clumsy
Arrogant	Callous	Conceited
Belligerent	Childish	Cynical

(Continued)

Dependent	Insecure	Short-tempered
Dishonest	Insensitive	Stubborn
Disorganised	Intolerant	Submissive
Disrespectful	Irresponsible	Suspicious
Distrustful	Jealous	Thoughtless
Egocentric	Malicious	Uncooperative
Envious	Manipulative	Undisciplined
Fearful	Moody	Unfriendly
Foolish	Nervous	Unimaginative
Forgetful	Neglectful	Unpredictable
Greedy	Opinionated	Unreliable
Gullible	Pessimistic	Unstable
Harsh	Prejudiced	Vain
Hostile	Reckless	Vindictive
Impatient	Rigid	Weak
Impulsive	Sceptical	Withdrawn
Indecisive	Selfish	
Inflexible	Shallow	

This isn't about beating yourself up – it's about honest self-awareness.

Ask:

- Which of these traits do I find hardest to deal with in others?
- Which ones have *I* been known to slip into under pressure?
- If I'm really honest: which one might a colleague quietly use to describe me?

Then reflect:

- When does that trait show up?
- What's underneath it – stress? Fear? Overwhelm?
- What would help me spot it and shift gears next time?

This step takes courage – but it's where genuine growth lives.

Step 6: Look at the Unknown Area

Now revisit Figure 3.1. Which adjectives has *no one* chosen – but you're curious about?

Maybe you've never been called *visionary* or *inspiring* – yet. But could you grow into those traits with confidence, support, or new opportunities?

The unknown area holds potential. How might you actively cultivate these qualities in yourself?

The Johari window should act as a compassionate, curious look at how we show up in our work and our relationships. Used well, it can be transformative.

CONCLUSION

The relationships we build within the school environment are fundamental to our professional success and personal wellbeing. Whether it's fostering positive connections with students or cultivating supportive networks among colleagues, these relationships form the backbone of a thriving educational community. As we navigate the complexities of our roles, it's essential to remember that building and maintaining these connections requires an investment of time and effort, and a consistent presence. By valuing and investing in these relationships, we not only enhance our own experience but also contribute to a more inclusive, collaborative, and supportive school culture.

REFERENCES

Collie, R. J., Shapka, J. D. and Perry, N. E. (2012). 'School climate and social-emotional learning: Predicting teacher stress, job satisfaction, and teaching efficacy'. *Journal of Educational Psychology, 104*(4), 1189–1204.

Cornelius-White, J. (2007). 'Learner-centered teacher-student relationships are effective: A meta-analysis'. *Review of Educational Research, 77*(1), 113–143.

Day, C. and Gu, Q. (2010). *The new lives of teachers*. Routledge.

Hughes, J. N. (2011). 'Longitudinal effects of teacher and student perceptions of teacher–student relationship qualities on academic adjustment'. *The Elementary School Journal, 112*(1), 38–60.

Luft, J. and Ingham, H. (1955). 'The Johari window, a graphic model of interpersonal awareness'. Proceedings of the Western Training Laboratory in Group Development. Los Angeles: University of California, Los Angeles.

Pianta, R. C., Hamre, B. K. and Allen, J. P. (2012). 'Teacher-student relationships and engagement: Conceptualizing, measuring, and improving the capacity of classroom interactions'. In S. Christenson, A. L. Reschly and C. Wylie (Eds.), *Handbook of Research on Student Engagement* (pp. 365–386). Springer.

Roorda, D. L., Koomen, H. M. Y., Spilt, J. L. and Oort, F. J. (2011). 'The influence of affective teacher–student relationships on students' school engagement and achievement: A meta-analytic approach'. *Review of Educational Research, 81*(4), 493–529.

Tschannen-Moran, M. (2009). Fostering teacher professionalism: The role of professional orientation and trust. *Educational Administration Quarterly, 45*(2), 217–247.

4

TEACHING DURING CHALLENGING TIMES

This chapter explores the challenges facing educators at macro, meso and micro levels, including:

- **Teaching during challenging times:** Exploring the impact of historical and societal contexts on the teaching profession, including global turbulence such as the pandemic, the cost of living, and war.
- **Perceptions and wellbeing:** Understanding how perceptions of teachers influence their engagement, wellbeing, recruitment, and retention.
- **Balancing life and teaching:** Reflecting on the challenges educators face in balancing their professional responsibilities with personal life demands.

MY STORY

It's 7 July 2005. I've taught Year 7, then Year 8 (a rather raucous lesson on animals, as I remember). As I head down to the staffroom for break, I notice 8 missed calls on my old Nokia. It's my husband. He's a journalist. The TV in the staffroom shows news of a gas explosion in London, not far from our school. When I call him, he tells me to tell the headteacher to keep the children in school – it's a terrorist attack, he says. It was, of course, the London bombings which have marked such a grimly significant point in our country's recent history. There's a sense of unreality but we focus on what we instinctively know matters most until late into the evening, staff who don't need to get home to their own families stay and ensure every child and parent is safely accounted for. I remember a profound sense of what it really means to be a teacher. It's not about the German word for guinea pig. It's about keeping children safe, providing calm, structure and sanctuary.

LAYERS OF INFLUENCE

To broach this somewhat daunting chapter, I have turned to Uri Bronfenbrenner's ecological theory model, on which I first drew for my doctoral studies. It depicts the layers of influence on educators' sense of identity, wellbeing and sense of self-efficacy as follows:

> Macro – the wider political, cultural and historical context of the role, including world events, government policies, the news and developments in society.

> Meso – your profession and personal communities; issues closer to home that have a direct impact on your ability to do your role properly, including school policies and procedures, expectations of performance, working hours, performance appraisals and the curriculum. These might also include relationships with stakeholders, especially parents, and issues affecting your local community.

> Micro – your immediate personal and professional relationships; the people and events which influence you closely on a regular basis. Your values and sense of identity.

When I wrote *How to Survive in Teaching* in 2017, I genuinely believed that the challenges for those working in schools were as bad as they were going to get – we'd already been facing a recruitment and retention crisis for years, teachers felt woefully under-supported by government and media and the statistics for poor mental health amongst school staff were alarming (Kell, 2018, p.9–41). This feels darkly, laughably naïve as I write today, and I must dig deep to hold onto my stubborn optimism as I embark on this chapter.

Dwelling too much in dark and difficult spaces risks sucking us into a spiral of despair, so I'd ask my readers to process this chapter with the same attitude in which I am writing it – coming from the point of view that there will always be children, and that children will always need teachers, and when the world is frightening and turbulent, our potential to add value is all the greater. When I work with educators, I always take time to acknowledge the challenges they face, and, whilst it's sobering, I have noticed that there is often a glint in their eyes: yes, it's tough. But I have the skills, the passion and the determination to make a difference, so *bring it on*!

I firmly believe that if we can give the difficulties a name, a shape, a texture, we have taken the first step to carving out ways of overcoming them, working around them, and reminding ourselves that we are not alone with the spiky, heavy burdens so many of us carry today.

Reflection: Barriers and Obstacles to Your Professional Wellbeing

Without over-thinking it, make a list of some of the things that make it hard for you to feel happy and fulfilled in your work – these can be anything from minor, irritating niggles to the big questions that wake you in the early hours of the morning. You can include references to individuals, but you may wish to write these in code in case anyone borrows your copy of the book!

Now, draw three concentric circles like the ones in Figure 4.1. Can you organise your challenges into each of the circles? (You may wish to refer back to the definitions of macro, meso and micro at the beginning of this chapter.)

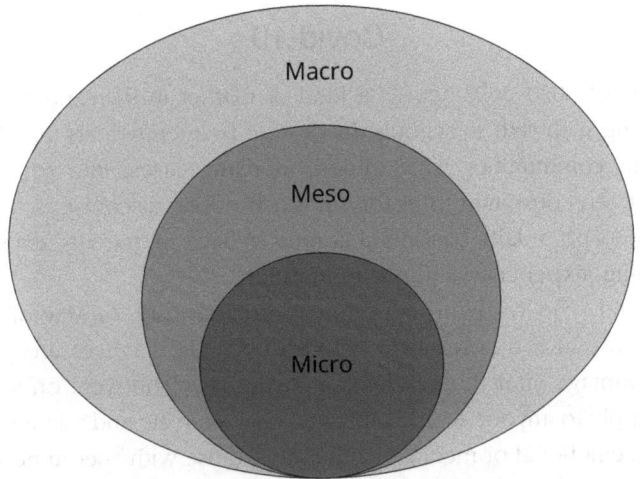

Figure 4.1   Mapping the challenges

Now have a think about *how much control* you have on each of the challenges you have identified. We'll discuss control in more depth in Chapter 5, but the key here is, as far as possible, making peace with the things we can't control and putting our energy into exerting maximum control in the areas where we can – and where it matters. Now, for each of your challenges, add a score of 1-10.

1: I have no control whatsoever over this.

10: I have maximum control over this and can change/shape it for the better.

So, if you are concerned about indications of toxic masculinity you've heard in your school, this might be a 7 – depending on your role in the school, you can raise your concerns, get together with others to propose ways of educating young people, seek out examples of good practice and see and intervention through these methods.

If one of your concerns is war, or the state of the environment, this might be nearer a 2 – you can control how you respond, how you communicate, whether you take personal responsibility for key actions such as fundraising, but you can't directly influence the outcomes.

There's no quality judgement related to high or low scores – it's just about thinking about your sphere of influence and starting to think about how you can use the control you have for maximum impact.

A whole book (or series of books) would be needed to give full justice to all the challenges in education at the moment, but in this chapter, I outline the ones that come to me through meeting hundreds of educators every year, in the UK and internationally.

MACRO FACTORS AFFECTING SCHOOLS

This section will explore the 'macro' or wider events that affect schools.

Covid-19

The pandemic of 2020–2022 acts as a kind of marker in the sand whenever I talk about wellbeing with staff in schools. In short, it frequently feels that the 'gaps' that existed in our communities have turned, in many cases, into gaping crevasses. Whilst it has been consigned to history in much public discourse, schools continue to feel its effects on a daily basis in children's behaviour, parents' expectations and gaps in learning, experience and communication.

A wise friend who works in educational research said, in May of 2020, 'if you were in any way at a disadvantage before Covid, the chances are you'll be at a greater disadvantage after the pandemic is over.' This, she went on to say, has the potential to apply to anyone with a protected characteristic and might apply to those with physical, emotional or mental health issues, those with special needs and those of lower socio-economic status. Her prediction has been borne out by much of what I've seen and heard when visiting schools and working with educators.

UCL's *Covid-19 Social Study* (Fancourt et al., 2023) shines a powerful light on the impact of the virus. Here are some of the most striking findings pertinent to those working in schools:

- Worry about – or direct experience of – loss of income, loss of work, challenges accessing essentials, and bereavement had negative effects on mental health (p.7).
- Those who were already vulnerable before Covid suffered disproportionately and their mental health was slower to recover than for other groups. This included women, young adults, people of lower educational attainment, and those living alone or with children; these groups also had slower rates of recovery (p.8).
- Psychological challenges were experienced by people with lower household income, educational qualifications or employment status, people from ethnic minority groups, adolescents, young adults, women, parents of young children, people with health conditions and key workers (p.8).
- Those who struggled with finances or employment were more likely to struggle even more during the pandemic (p.8).

If we reflect on these findings in the context of schools, it helps to contextualise many of the challenges our communities continue to experience, from the haemorrhaging of support staff (whose income is often very low) to challenges when engaging parents, to manifestations of anxiety and poor mental health. Where, prior to Covid, schools could focus their energies on a small minority of families or colleagues experiencing financial hardship or poor mental health, these issues are now widespread, affecting people from all groups, from our students, to our senior leaders, to our parents, to the colleagues in the classroom next door.

Case Study: Greg

Life After the Pandemic – A Deputy Headteacher's Perspective

As a deputy headteacher in a large primary school in the Midlands, I've witnessed first-hand how the lasting impact of the pandemic continues to shape our school environment – even now, in 2025. While the national narrative has largely moved on, for those of us working in schools, the ripple effects are far from over.

One of the most significant shifts we've seen is the sharp rise in pupils with complex needs. The number of children on our SEND register has grown year on year, and many present with challenges that don't fit neatly into existing categories. Teachers are constantly adapting their practice to meet a wide range of needs, often with limited access to specialist support due to ongoing delays in referrals and stretched external services.

Alongside this, we've noticed a change in parental expectations. Post-pandemic anxiety and a desire to see their children 'catch up' have fuelled a rise in pressure from parents – emails questioning lesson content, demands for personalised feedback, and concerns raised through increasingly formal channels. There's a sense that some families view teachers as solely responsible for repairing the damage caused by years of disrupted learning, and it's becoming overwhelming for staff.

Challenging behaviour has also become more frequent and more complex. Many pupils are still dealing with the emotional fallout of those formative years spent in isolation, or within unpredictable home environments. We're seeing more incidents of dysregulation and emotional outbursts – particularly among children who missed out on vital early social and emotional development. Managing behaviour now takes up a significant part of the school day, and this adds another layer of stress to already stretched staff. I took this role with a clear vision and commitment to strategy but I feel as if I'm firefighting most days!

All of this is happening in a climate of mounting accountability. The pressure to raise attendance rates has intensified in the past year, with schools being closely monitored by local authorities and trusts. There's an expectation that we challenge absences robustly, regardless of the context. While we absolutely value high attendance, the nuance of individual family circumstances can be lost in the drive to meet national benchmarks.

We're doing what we can – offering wellbeing check-ins, flexible working options, and trying to reduce unnecessary workload – but the cumulative impact is undeniable. Teachers are tired. Some are questioning whether they can sustain this pace and intensity much longer. It's clear that if we're to retain our skilled workforce, there needs to be a genuine, system-wide commitment to supporting the people who keep our schools going. The challenges of 2025 are no longer about 'recovery', they're about survival and sustainability in a new educational reality.

Reflection: Challenges Facing Your School

Can you relate to the challenges Greg describes? Are there others that your school is facing that he hasn't mentioned? What impact have they had on you and your colleagues?

Information Overload

We exist in an age where information is ubiquitous – how many of us reach for our phone as soon as we wake up to plug back into the bombardment of news and updates and end our waking hours with a quick check of our work email or a scan of the news? The result is that we frequently feel overwhelmed and overloaded with information. As Hari puts it in his excellent book, *Stolen Focus*:

> In 1986, if you added up all the information being blasted at the average human being – TV, radio, reading – it amounted to forty newspapers-worth of information every day. By 2007, they found it had risen to the equivalent of 174 newspapers per day. (I'd be amazed if it hadn't gone up further since then.) The increase in the volume of information is what creates the sensation of the world speeding up. (2022, p.30)

Add to this the fact that most educators are surrounded by dozens of young people every day, each with their own unique needs and expectations of us, and required to perform according to a set of expectations, and it's not surprising if our brains often start to fizz.

Whilst, of course, a video about a daft golden retriever, or a wise and uplifting blog, or a powerful new contact can enrich and enhance us, repeated demands on our attention can and do have a serious impact on us. The concept of 'doom scrolling' is a powerful one – you are convinced the world is going to hell in a handcart and something in your brain tells you to continue to absorb information that confirms this theory, and the spiral begins – the negativity bias in full action!

Reflection: Negative Effects of Media and Social Media

Over the next few days, be actively mindful of your exposure to media in all its forms (from TV to the internet) and tune into the times when this is unhelpful to you – it might raise your stress/anxiety levels, fuel a sense of injustice, reduce your attention span, disturb your sleep, give you 'decision fatigue' or decrease your productivity. This activity is about noticing and being aware – once you're aware, you have more power to make choices.

- Raised levels of stress and anxiety. Example: Local Facebook tells us there are thefts in the area; Ofsted is in the school down the road…
- An increased sense of injustice. Example: Someone has spotted an unexpected caravan in the next village and others are making discriminatory comments about the Traveller community; someone has slated the teaching profession online…
- Reduced attention span. Example: Dinner was burned because you were doing a 'quick check' of your school email; you didn't pay attention to a family member because you were distracted by your beeping phone…
- Sleep disturbances. Example: Waking up and checking your email in case your colleague has replied to your urgent email, sent before bed…
- Decreased productivity. Example; Doing a piece of work that requires sustained concentration but finding yourself regularly pulled back to check your social media or emails.

This activity isn't designed to make you feel guilty or bad about the impact of information overload – as Johann Hari says in *Stolen Focus*, 'it's not your fault you can't focus' – those beeps and flags on your phone are cunningly *designed* to distract you – but, as with all habits, if we can be mindful of their impact on us, we have more power to change them for the better.

To balance this activity, I'd also encourage you to make a note of the times when media and social media are actively helpful to you – bringing laughter, useful contacts, helpful research or resources or genuinely relaxing distraction. Make a note of these in the box below.

Conflict, Climate Change, Intolerance and Extremism

At the time of writing, our world is fraught with war and conflict and rhetoric from our leaders seems to fuel division and conflict. Environmental disaster is looming, there is a global financial crisis and the pieces we have left this next generation to pick up feel so broken and so scattered. Toxic masculinity and extremism seem to be on the rise and young people grapple to form a sense of identity amidst the noise of social media and the lack of answers from their elders. Making time for healthy communication and debate to ensure young people have a voice is key, and yet the ongoing hyper-accountability of schools means that data and exam results have such high stakes that this time and space is squeezed to almost nothing.

Recruitment and Retention

When I first started researching teacher wellbeing over ten years ago now, there was a recruitment crisis in teaching. In fact, I struggle to remember a point in my career when there hasn't been some kind of crisis. I got my first job during a dearth of MFL teachers in 1999. Today, I speak to headteachers who tell me that they've put ads out for Geography teachers and had literally no applications – 'I'd just like to receive something, so I have something to read!' said one.

Data from the National Federation for Educational Research (NFER) indicates that teacher recruitment remains stubbornly below targets in most subjects and retention has not improved since the pandemic (McLean and Worth, 2025). Many young people here in the UK are being taught by non-specialist or unqualified teachers.

In my early years of teaching, school leadership felt like the holy grail of ambitions – the most noble, influential role we could each aspire to reach, but the attraction of the role has clearly lost its shine. Recent research from the NAHT (2022) shows that only 30% of existing school leaders would recommend school leadership as a career choice, 31% left their post within five years, and of these, 52% left state-funded schools altogether.

The crisis is affecting our support staff too. Moral purpose and a love of working with children hasn't been enough to keep many of our invaluable teaching assistants in the classroom – these people are often the heart and lungs of a school, frequently with excellent knowledge of the local community; they're the ones who patiently work alongside our children with the most profound needs, offering reassurance and support to students, teachers and families. Most of the primary schools I've visited in the last year talk of a shortage: 'She went to work in Starbucks alongside her son,' said a headteacher of one long-serving teaching assistant. 'She gets paid more there.' In a cost-of-living crisis, with bills to pay and families to feed, the woefully low rate of pay for our support staff mean our students are missing out on a truly precious resource (Fazackerley, 2023).

As if it couldn't be any worse, it is perhaps unsurprising that schools in disadvantaged areas are hit hardest by the recruitment and retention crisis (Henshaw, 2022), meaning our most vulnerable young people are the ones most likely to miss out and exacerbating the 'gaps' – or crevasses – in our society.

The dismal and worrying picture in the UK is reflected in the international picture, with UNESCO's *Global Report on Teachers* revealing the urgent need for 44 million primary and secondary teachers worldwide by 2030 (UNESCO, 2024).

David Edwards, General Secretary of Education International summarises the crisis as follows:

> *Today, teachers are overworked, undervalued and underpaid, and more and more are forced to leave the profession. At the same time, fewer young people aspire to be teachers. It's easy to see why. Working conditions have deteriorated, pay has not kept up with inflation, workloads have skyrocketed, and professional autonomy has been steadily replaced with never-ending controls and bureaucracy.* (Edwards, 2023)

Teacher pay still compares unfavourably to many other professions, here in the UK (Worth, 2023) and internationally, where it is lower than for other professions requiring equivalent levels of qualification (OECD, 2023). Limited options for flexible working remain an issue – where other sectors have embraced opportunities for flexible working since the pandemic, schools have been slower to catch-on (Gould, 2023).

Growing Levels of Need

Schools worldwide are reporting that meeting the needs of all of their learners (one of the basic teachers' standards here in the UK) is becoming increasingly difficult. This isn't surprising when we consider the impact of the pandemic on young people; mental health issues abound and parents report waiting lists which frequently exceed two years for children who are experiencing self-harm or eating disorders. There's a similarly long wait for diagnoses of special educational needs, with 'thresholds' for specialist support seeming to rise out of reach of many mainstream schools. The result is often a situation where there are no winners – children are in classrooms with teachers who simply don't have the capacity to meet their needs. When children's needs aren't being met – in most cases through no fault of any individual – they can quite literally lash out. I'm seeing and hearing of more and more school staff leaving sites with physical injuries resulting from behaviours of students who are distressed and seriously dysregulated, including one coaching client who ended up with a broken nose when trying to split up a fight.

Workload

Workload is a perennial problem in schools and has been since I started teaching. The nature of the job means that it is literally never 'done' – there's always more to do! Here in the UK, some measures have been taken to acknowledge the toll of the workload on school staff and to put in place reasonable measures around tasks like marking and paperwork. But it strikes me whenever I meet with school staff that the issue runs more deeply than this, because teaching has become so much more than just curriculum and pedagogy. There's always been a strong pastoral focus here in the UK (and I amongst many of my colleagues welcome this – trust and relationships are central to helping students thrive as whole human beings) and there's always been an element of social work, counselling, nursing in our role. But, where other services closed their doors during the pandemic, ours remained open – at the very least to our most vulnerable children and families. Despite the challenges, it's fair to assert that educators and schools are perceived for the most part by communities as a source of information, reassurance, and support. 'With all other doors closed, we've become marriage guidance counsellors, financial advisors, shoe-fitters and nutrition experts!' said one deputy headteacher.

As a profession, we are good at problem-solving, relating to people and getting things done – so, whether it's tracking sexual violence, supervising tooth brushing or providing advice on sleep routines, schools have stepped in, rolled their sleeves up and got on with it. Whatever balls have been thrown at us, for all the challenges, we have caught them and dealt with them – but how sustainable is this?

Moral Purpose and Compassion Stress

People who come into the profession have a strong sense of purpose. We've got gold dust in our hands and all they want to do is teach. But we take bright shiny people and grind the life out of them. It's an incredible own goal. (Sinéad McBrearty, CEO of Education Support, Labour Party Conference 2023)

There comes a point at which the spark which led us to yearn to make a difference becomes a raging furnace that threatens to consume us. Making a difference feels good, so we keep doing it – and we keep doing it again, and we fend off the balls firing at us until our own self-care seems to fall to the very bottom of the list of priorities.

Working with children with increasingly profound and complex needs takes its toll on adults too, as highlighted by Dr Rachel Briggs in her doctoral thesis (2021). Compassion is at the heart of our sense of moral purpose, for many of us in education, but the snake can end up eating its own tail. In a conversation with me in 2022, Rachel put it like this:

Fundamentally, compassion is the desire to 'connect with someone's distress and want to alleviate it'. Where 'compassion satisfaction' is achieved, the desire to 'make a difference' is fulfilled, which results in high levels of job satisfaction and wellbeing. However with the cumulative impact of feeling you're taking on others' distress but are powerless to help, 'compassion injury' can set in, with symptoms akin to those of PTSD.

Reflection: The Impact of the Challenges on You and Your Colleagues

The account of challenges at macro level provided in this chapter obviously isn't exhaustive – we'd require a book (or series of books) to do this subject justice. Take a few minutes, alone or with your team, to reflect on how national and international developments have impacted on your work in schools – try to be as factual and dispassionate as possible. What is empirically true in terms of incidents dealt with, hours worked, staffing capacity, etc.? This exercise isn't designed to depress you but perhaps to help you understand the factors behind the exhaustion and frustration you and your colleagues may be feeling.

MESO FACTORS AFFECTING SCHOOL STAFF

This section outlines some of the factors at 'meso' level which challenge school staff; community norms and practices, policies and communication and networks.

Missing in Action

The realities of working in an under-staffed school mean that stress levels are exacerbated for everyone at the chalkface – and added to the cocktail of the recruitment and retention crisis is a spike in staff absence, which has risen by 56% since the pandemic (Whittaker, 2023). It's hard to pin down precise data when it comes to whether these absences are down to physical or mental health issues (or a combination of the two!), but stress and workload do appear to play a significant role in this issue.

The true impact of missing staff on those who need to hold the fort is massive, and the deep irony is that absence is 'catching' – in every sense of the word. Put the rest of the stuff under enough pressure, and they risk hitting breaking point too, as we see from our next case study.

Case Study: Maryam

I've Never Felt as if I Were Doing Such a Bad Job

Maryam's no longer in teaching. Up until recently, she was Head of Maths in a school in the North of England. 'I used to love my job!' she told me. 'I was good at it – at least I think I was. Hang on…' Maryam fumbles in a box and pulls out a card from a student, received on her last day. 'Thank you for not giving up on me,'

(Continued)

---

it says, simply. 'This student used to tell me he hated me!' she says with a wry smile. 'But I was stubborn. I refused to give up on him – I knew he could do it.'

Maryam was really proud of the team she'd built up over the years. 'It was a mess to start with,' she said. 'But we worked together to make it better – we had some of the best results in the school and I was so proud of my team!' The first couple of major absences hit after Covid – one staff member had long Covid and had been away from school for three months when I first met Maryam. Another staff member had a bereavement and struggled to get through a school day without breaking down – sometimes in front of students. 'It was cruel not to let her go home,' said Maryam. 'I tried to get her support but I still worry about her every day.' A third member of the team of six was diagnosed with cancer and had to be off for long periods.

The daily reality for Maryam went from enacting her strategic vision with her team to 'pure firefighting'. 'I had to set cover for around 25 different classes every single day. I was running around, dealing with behaviour issues, delivering books – whilst I was supposed to be teaching my own exam classes! I've never worked so hard in my life – and I've never felt as if I were doing such a bad job.'

Maryam has a reputation for being efficient and effective – asking for help didn't come naturally, but she let her line manager know she was struggling. 'Nothing changed,' she said. 'They told me they knew they were in "safe hands" with me and just let me get on with it.'

Maryam has high expectations and high aspirations for herself and her students – as we would expect of any teacher. Her sense of self-efficacy – and the sheer volume of the workload – took their toll. 'One day I found myself shaking so hard in the car on the way to school that I didn't think I'd be able to get through the day.' Sleep disturbance, missed meals, panic attacks ensued – her partner was worried; her doctor was worried. Nothing changed. So she handed in her resignation.

I hear stories like Maryam's every week – more and more of them. Excellent teachers, dedicated professionals with the desire and talent to inspire young people who are made to work in impossible sets of circumstances. For the sake of her health and her family, Maryam had to walk away. Whether she will return to the teaching profession or not remains to be seen.

Matching Your Values to Your School

For school staff – as explored in depth in *How to Survive* (2018) – finding a school where your values are aligned (see Chapter 2 for more on values) is key. This will be apparent in relationships, communication, policies and procedures and 'norms' in your school. This isn't an exact science – we all have to be flexible at times, but if you are passionate about inclusion, it's important that your school's policies and practices support this – ask about it at interview!

If you feel your values are regularly being challenged, it's worth quite literally scheduling 'check in' points with yourself – if it's dark and cold and you're feeling a bit under the weather, it might not be the day to resign, but make a vow to check in with yourself a few weeks down the line. Talking to someone you trust; journaling – all of these can help you gain clarity. As I've discussed in other work, I learned the hard way that persisting in trying to fit your square peg into the round hole of an organisation can ultimately make you ill.

Communication, Calendars and Meetings

How to Survive (2018) goes into detail into the number of factors which can bring staff down in individual organisations, but it's worth highlighting here the damaging effects of disorganised – or badly organised – calendars (I've known schools with two parents' evenings, marking deadlines and twilight CPD falling in the same fortnight). Remembering that 'what's urgent for you isn't necessarily urgent for me' (middle leader) is important – people resent last-minute demands and extra pressure. And meetings – I have an abiding memory of having a tiny daughter with the childminder while a meeting, due to finish at 4.30, crept towards 4.40 with a debate about literacy codes, then towards 4.50 – I thought I'd vomit with stress as I remembered the line in the childminder's contract which said that they'd call social services if a parent was more than half an hour late for pick-up… Always finish meetings on time!

Emotional Contagion

When people are struggling with anxiety about the state of the world and carrying heavy, prickly burdens of their own, from money worries to bereavement, they don't always behave in ways that are optimal for staff morale – and this is forgivable – the need for having space for vulnerability in your school's culture is clear. But when they start to perceive others as a threat, become resistant to necessary change, create cliques and fuel hostility, this can make the day-to-day job intolerable for others.

Reflection: Challenges to Your Values

Refer back to your values compass from Chapter 1. Use it to reflect on the following:

Think of an occasion recently when an element of your work left you feeling frustrated or upset or angry. Which of your values was being challenged? What impact did it have on you?

Now think of an occasion when you felt genuinely proud of an element of your job. Which of your values was being lived out?

MICRO FACTORS AFFECTING STAFF IN SCHOOLS

Now we move on to exploring the 'micro' factors affecting staff in schools.

Personal Challenges

The personal challenges of staff in schools are often precisely what fuels their desire to work with young people – 'I just wanted to give them the experience I never had,' said one teacher, who described feeling 'invisible' in schools. The sheer richness of human experience means that our learning from such challenges can make us better teachers and better leaders.

Through the privilege of working as a coach, I have a glimpse into the complexities behind the smiling, confident facades of so many of our colleagues in schools. And, of course, school staff are not immune to the effects of the challenges cited earlier in this chapter, from financial worries, to mental health issues, to the concerning rise in domestic violence.

The best mantra is to assume that you don't know a fraction of what is going on behind the scenes for your colleagues. Have a look at our next case study for an example of a teacher who shared her story with me.

Case Study: Leanne

'I will never again judge a parent for the conduct of their child,' said a senior leader I spoke to for this research. Her own child, brought up on a diet of literature and travel, had become involved in County Lines. They were currently 'proofing' their house, on the police's advice, against the threat of retaliation after he allegedly 'stole some weed'. 'The anxiety is unbearable,' she said. 'What did I do wrong? I find being in work a comfort – at least I know what's expected of me here. I just hope I've instilled in him the tools and values to get through this.'

Perfectionism

Perfectionism is a trait held by many in our profession – the need to 'get it right' can mean that hours more are spent poring over lesson plans and marking than is (arguably) strictly necessary and the inner voice that says that you have to do the best job you possibly can means than no number of reasonable policies around workload are going to stop you working until 2 am when the urge takes you. A colleague, who calls herself a 'recovering perfectionist' says she has to hold on to the 'good enough' mantra and force herself to walk away – she's placed strict limits on her working hours and ('it goes against all my instincts!') and forces herself to adopt the attitude of 'I've got this – it will be what it will be!'

The bottom line is that no child or teenager is going to thank you for staying up half the night refining the PowerPoint presentation or worksheet you are preparing for them.

Guilt and Shame

As difference-makers fuelled by moral purpose, those of us who work in schools can be especially susceptible to feelings of guilt. 'I just got sick of feeling I was letting everyone down all of the time,' said a former teacher and mother to me during my research for my doctorate – 'I couldn't bear the feeling that I was doing so many things and not doing any of them properly.' Having to say 'no' to a parent who desperately wants their child's seat moved in the classroom (for the sixth time this year) or to a colleague who's requested three days off to go to a relative's wedding overseas can leave staff feeling that they're in a no-win situation.

Guilt over being distracted when you last visited your mum, forgetting to take the cat to the vet, not making it to your friend's hen do because you were just too shattered, not noticing that a colleague was distressed, forgetting an important deadline... these can pile up and distil into a more pernicious sense of inferiority and judgement.

The Toll on Mental Health and Wellbeing

It's rare to find a lazy person working in a school – whether you're the business manager, a teaching assistant or a middle leader, frankly, you could take your significant range of skills into many other sectors. We don't choose to work in schools for an easy life, and we expect (even hope) to be challenged and to learn and grow. But when does the level of challenge become too much?

Education Support, a charity based here in the UK, has undertaken an annual survey since 2017. This has demonstrated powerfully that teachers experience significantly higher rates of stress, anxiety and depression than the general population. In 2024, it found that the behaviour of students and demands of parents were significant factors contributing to teacher stress.

From headteacher Ruth Perry, who took her own life in the wake of an 'unsatisfactory' Ofsted inspection, to my own headteacher, Kevin McKellar (Kell, 2014), we witness far too often the devastation and the ultimate tragedy that can come from hitting rock bottom and the ripple effects that last for generations.

It's my moral imperative – and I would urge you to join me – to take all the measures we can to ensure others don't pay this ultimate price.

FOR LEADERS: MANAGING THE CHALLENGES

1 **Acknowledge the challenges:** Recognise the various levels of challenges (macro, meso and micro) that educators face. This includes understanding the

impact of global events, societal changes, and personal circumstances on teachers' wellbeing.

2   **Foster a supportive environment:** Create a culture of support within the school. This can involve offering wellbeing check-ins, flexible working options, and reducing unnecessary workload to help staff manage stress and maintain their mental health.

3   **Encourage open communication:** Promote open and honest communication among staff. This helps in addressing issues promptly and ensures that everyone feels heard and valued.

4   **Provide professional development:** Offer opportunities for professional growth and development. This can help teachers feel more confident and capable in their roles, which can reduce stress and improve job satisfaction.

5   **Promote work–life balance:** Encourage staff to maintain a healthy work–life balance. This can involve setting clear boundaries around work hours and providing resources to help staff manage their time effectively.

By implementing these strategies, leaders can help create a supportive and positive environment for educators, which can ultimately benefit the entire school community.

CONCLUSION

In this chapter, we have delved into the myriad challenges faced by educators in recent times, from the global turbulence of the pandemic to the societal and personal pressures that impact educators' daily lives. We have explored the historical and societal contexts influencing the teaching profession, the perceptions of teachers, and the balancing act between teaching and wider life demands.

While this chapter has undoubtedly presented some of the darkest aspects of the teaching profession, rest assured that this is the low point of the book! From here on, pragmatism and positivity will abound. The resilience and determination of educators to make a difference, despite the challenges, will shine through. As we move forward, we will focus on practical strategies and positive approaches that can help navigate these turbulent times and bring about meaningful change.

REFERENCES

Briggs, R. (2021). *What about me? Teachers' psychological wellbeing and how it can be supported when teaching pupils experiencing vulnerabilities and/or trauma* (Thesis). University of Bristol. https://research-information.bris.ac.uk/ws/portalfiles/portal/281718007/Final_Copy_2021_07_01_Briggs_R_EdD.pdf

Education Support (2024). *Teacher wellbeing index*. November. www.educationsupport.org.uk/resources/for-organisations/research/teacher-wellbeing-index/

Edwards, D. (2023). 'Addressing the teacher shortage – a global imperative'. *United Nations, UN Chronicle*. www.un.org/en/un-chronicle/addressing-teacher-shortage%E2%80%94-global-imperative

Fancourt, D., Bu, F., Paul, E. and Steptoe, A. (2023). *COVID-19 Social Study, April 2020-December 2023*. Nuffield Foundation. https://www.nuffieldfoundation.org/project/covid-19-social-study

Fazackerley, A. (2023). 'Low pay "forcing teaching assistants out of UK classrooms"'. *The Guardian*, 14 May. www.theguardian.com/education/2023/may/14/low-pay-teaching-assistants-uk-classrooms

Gould, M. (2023). 'Lack of flexible working "putting off potential teachers"'. *TES Magazine*, 30 June. www.tes.com/magazine/news/general/lack-flexible-working-potential-teacher-trainees-itt

Hari, J. (2022). *Stolen focus: Why you can't pay attention – and how to think deeply again*. Crown Publishing Group.

Henshaw, P. (2022). 'Recruitment and retention: The most deprived schools hit hardest'. *SecEd*, 7 December. www.sec-ed.co.uk/content/news/recruitment-and-retention-the-most-deprived-schools-hit-hardest/

Kell, E. (2014). 'Losing your head.' 27 August. https://thosethatcanteach.wordpress.com/2014/08/27/losing-your-head/

Kell, E. (2018). *How to survive in teaching: Without imploding, exploding or walking away*. Bloomsbury.

McLean, D. and Worth, J. (2025). *Teacher labour market in England annual report 2025*. National Federation for Educational Research, 13 March. www.nfer.ac.uk/publications/teacher-labour-market-in-england-annual-report-2025/

National Association of Head Teachers (NAHT) (2022). *Gone for good: Leaders who are lost to the teacher profession*. November. http://naht.org.uk/Portals/0/PDF's/Campaigns/NAHT-Retention-rate-report-FINAL.pdf

Organisation for Economic Co-operation and Development (OECD) (2023). 'Education indicators in focus: What do OECD data on teachers' salaries tell us? October. www.oecd.org/content/dam/oecd/en/publications/reports/2023/10/what-do-oecd-data-on-teachers-salaries-tell-us_449e60c7/de0196b5-en.pdf

United Nations Educational, Scientific and Cultural Organization (UNESCO) (2024). *Global report on teachers: Addressing teacher shortages and transforming the profession*. https://teachertaskforce.org/sites/default/files/2024-04/2349-23_GlobalReportonTeacher_WEB.pd

Whittaker, F. (2023). 'Teacher sickness absence soars in wake of pandemic'. *SchoolsWeek*, 8 June. https://schoolsweek.co.uk/teacher-sickness-absence-soars-in-wake-of-pandemic/#:~:text=The%20number%20of%20teachers'%20working,maternity%20leave%20or%20career%20breaks

Worth, J. (2023). *Addressing the post-pandemic teacher recruitment and retention challenges in England*. NFER, June. www.nuffieldfoundation.org/wp-content/uploads/2023/05/Addressing-the-post-pandemic-teacher-recruitment-and-retention-challenges-in-England-Jack-Worth.pdf

5
NAVIGATING CHANGE

This chapter explores:

- The **impact of change** on the education system and school culture.
- Preparing students and educators for an **unpredictable future**.
- **Global trends** and key areas of **change in education**.
- The role of schools in providing **stability, security, and guidance** amidst change.
- The WHEELS model for **implementing change** in schools.

CHANGE, CHAOS AND THE ROLE OF SCHOOLS

Nobody joins the teaching profession for an uneventful professional existence. The truism that working in schools is 'never boring' is more apt than ever, as we navigate a flood of exponential change in the world and our collective and individual responses to it. The role of schools involves so much more than generating a decent set of professional qualifications for young people; at their most effective, the corridors, schools and outdoor spaces in schools provide a haven and an essential guide to our next generation, providing them with tools and templates to navigate towards a good life. Where there is danger, effective schools help equip children to remain safe; where there is turbulence, they provide stability; where there is confusion, they provide psychological security and guidance; where there is chaos, they provide routine and structure. Humans and the future are, in essence, unpredictable, but, when we do our jobs well, we use our intelligence and our experience to open pathways and equip students with the kit they need to live happy and successful lives.

Reflection: You and Your Impact

Let's build on your reflections from previous chapters. In your opinion as a professional, what, ultimately, is the role of a school and what is your unique role within that space? If you do your job effectively, what *impact* will you have on the young people you work with?

Our role as educators in shaping the next generation is an honour – the engagement and excitement of this journey can often make it feel like the best job in the world. We get to answer the big questions – 'What's the point of French, Miss?' 'Let me tell you...' 'Why do I need maths?' 'Well, let me begin...' 'How many tenses *are* there, Sir?' 'What if I flip this bottle really high...? Oh...' We function in a climate of curiosity and in it, we foster resilience and growth.

Global changes in technology, demographics and economic conditions place constant fresh demands on the world of education, posing urgent and often divisive questions around educational philosophy and the role of policy-makers and government. These have profound and ongoing implications for curriculum and pedagogy, the structure and management of schools, technological integration, wellbeing and special educational needs and professional development. When we say the job of educators is never 'done', we're really not joking...

Amidst the breakneck speed of change, we can never rest on our laurels and have to continually ask ourselves the biggest questions of all: given the developments and changes in the last year, day, hour, minute, in our young people themselves and the real and virtual communities they exist in, *how* do we prepare them for good lives?

In their pivotal and exciting project, *Future of Education and Skills 2030/2040*, the OECD asks these crucial questions:

> *How can we prepare students for jobs that have not yet been created, to tackle societal challenges that we can't yet imagine, and to use technologies that have not yet been invented? How can we equip them to thrive in an interconnected world where they need to understand and appreciate different perspectives and world views, interact respectfully with others, and take responsible action towards sustainability and collective wellbeing?* (OECD, 2024)

It's at our peril that we ignore such questions. There's a strong argument, says education consultant Karl Pupé in conversation with me in July 2024, that schools and educators are ill-equipped to prepare young people for an evolving and unknown future. Pupé quotes Warren Buffett as he reflects that the tide's in at the moment and we all look as if we're happily swimming away, but only when the tide goes out do you discover who's been swimming naked.

Pupé expands on this:

Unpopular opinion.

The education system is failing to prepare our students for the future.

The 40–40 plan (40 hours a week for 40 years of work) is dead.

According to this ABC report (Zahn, 2024), here's what might happen:

- *Up to nearly 8 million jobs could be eliminated by AI.*
- *Women and early-career employees are most at risk.*
- *11% of tasks are currently at risk of displacement by AI.*
- *High-risk jobs include entry-level, part-time, and administrative roles.*
- *One-third of administrative jobs could be eliminated soon.*
- *AI could displace 15% of workers (400 million people) worldwide by 2030.*

We are training our kids for a world that no longer exists.

We have to train our kids in a different way. Entrepreneurial skills are no longer a luxury but a necessity as job security wanes.

Our education system is the dinosaur that saw the glowing star in the sky coming closer every day...

As I discussed this issue with him, I found myself experience an unexpected roller coaster of emotions. Behind his humour, there's a sense of rage and despair, as he highlights the growing inequalities in our societies – 'those who are most up-to-date and best equipped to deal with the changes? The most wealthy. No s**t, Sherlock.'

I'm picturing the exhausted, harassed teacher racing to collect her kids before the childminder's shift ends, who can barely remember what she's supposed to be teaching Year 9 tomorrow, or how she's going to deal with the latest parental complaint, or fathom what she's going to feed her kids for dinner, let alone address existential questions over her role in preparing her students (and indeed her children) for the entirely unpreparable.

'I'm doing my best!' is a cry I hear regularly from educators everywhere, and I can't help but wonder if our current retention crisis is fuelled by a sense of impotent despair in the face of the deluge of change, alongside the issues around workload, conditions and pay discussed in Chapter 4. As an educator myself, I can relate to the rising feeling of 'stop the world, I want to get off – I just can't do any more than I'm doing already and I'm really not sure I can keep up.'

And, as the gremlin on my shoulder starts to demand that I back off and let someone more competent rise to the challenge, I realise the need to put my pragmatist's hat back on.

It turns out that, because of the breakneck speed of change in technology and the employment landscape, there are very few people who would actually dare to call themselves 'experts'; by the time they've completed any particular piece of research, things have already moved on far beyond their areas of expertise. In some ways, this realisation is accompanied by a bit of relief – it's like when we realise we're adults and that, basically, everyone else is making it up as they go along too!

Reflection: Consider Your Own School Experience

Which elements of it were most formative for your current self and role?

Whilst the mastery of a particular concept or skill or a sporting achievement may dominate for you, I'm willing to hazard that the vast majority of examples will involve human interaction. The teacher who implied you'd never amount to much who's been on your shoulder as you've regularly proved them wrong; the one who highlighted your talent in Music, Art, Drama or Science…

PREPARING OUR STUDENTS – AND OURSELVES – FOR AN UNPREDICTABLE FUTURE. WHAT DO WE NEED?

Case Study: 'We Don't Know What's Coming – But They'll Be Ready'

On a damp Wednesday afternoon, I visit a Humanities department where something special is happening. Lessons don't just deliver content – they develop people. 'We don't teach them for the world we had,' the head of department told me. 'We teach them for the world they'll shape.'

The curriculum is built around big questions: 'What does it mean to belong? Who decides what's fair?' designed to stretch thinking, spark empathy, and connect learning to real life. When the Ukraine conflict began, the team paused planned lessons so students could explore the crisis, ask questions, and lead fundraising efforts.

At the core of the department's approach are five key skills: **critical thinking, empathy, communication, adaptability**, and **collaboration** – what they call the *Future Five*. These run through everything they do, from debates and presentations to student-led campaigns.

The results go beyond grades. One former student, now in climate policy, wrote: 'What I remember most is how you made me feel my voice mattered.'

This team isn't pretending to predict the future. But they are raising young people who are ready to face it – with courage, compassion, and curiosity. And in these uncertain times, that's more than enough.

Whilst debate and sometimes unhelpful conflict abound in terms of how schools should go about preparing young people to live happy and successful lives, there is broad agreement on the key skills and competencies we need to foster as educators. There is a wealth of literature available in this area, but it merits an overview here, as we have established that educators need to feel successful – to have a sense of self-efficacy – to be most likely to remain happily and effectively in the profession.

Table 5.1 categorises the key skills and competencies likely to be needed by our young people as they become adults. The table offers an opportunity to reflect on how confident you feel in delivering in each of the areas. This may provide a helpful tool for planning your own professional development and that of your team as well as a starting point for a review of your curriculum offer. It's also important to note that what we *model* as the adults in the classrooms, corridors and offices is key here – children will always pick up on our actions, attitudes and comments.

Table 5.1 Key Skills and Competencies for Young People

Key skill or competence	Definition	How confident are you? What challenges are you facing? What support do you need?	How effectively are these covered in your school or team?
Fundamental skills			
Literacy and numeracy	These continue to provide the essential foundations on which future schools in work and life can be built.		
Digital literacy	The ability to use technology effectively to communicate, gather information and solve problems is increasingly vital.		

(Continued)

Table 5.1 (Continued)

Key skill or competence	Definition	How confident are you? What challenges are you facing? What support do you need?	How effectively are these covered in your school or team?
Critical thinking and problem-solving	The ability to analyse information (including evaluating its accuracy and validity) and develop effective approaches and actions is key.		
Creativity and Innovation	An area arguably neglected in UK education of late, the ability to foster new ideas and come up with new approaches is fundamental for our young people's personal and professional success.		
Interpersonal skills			
Communication	Effective verbal and written communication are essential for building relationships and collaborating effectively with others.		
Emotional Intelligence	Emotional self-regulation, management of the range of intensive emotions that come with living in our evolving world and developing healthy levels of empathy contribute to strong interpersonal connections.		
Teamwork and Collaboration	Students need to develop the ability to work effectively with a diverse range of other people in order to achieve common goals.		
Leadership	Teaching our young people to influence and inspire others is key.		

Key skill or competence	Definition	How confident are you? What challenges are you facing? What support do you need?	How effectively are these covered in your school or team?
		Life skills	
Resilience	Life is tricky. The ability to navigate, adapt to and learn from challenges and adversity is an essential skill that we can foster within and beyond schools.		
Time management and productivity	We are in receipt of so much information and *stuff* that teaching our young people how to efficiently manage time and resources is essential.		
Financial literacy	The ability to understand how money works, including budgeting and saving, is key.		
Global citizenship	During a period where intolerance, division and inequity are huge issues, developing a sense of responsibility for the world and understanding of different cultures is of utmost importance.		

BALANCING CHANGE WITH A REASONABLE WORKLOAD – AND THE EXPECTATIONS OF PARENTS, CARERS AND COMMUNITIES

As we've established in Chapter 4, workload is a huge factor in the teacher retention crisis and I must admit that, even (or especially) as a teacher with 26 years' experience, the list in Table 5.1 is pretty daunting. Financial literacy? Many teachers I know are struggling to stay on top of their own finances...

But the idea that the job of educators is simply to teach academic subjects is a distant memory. Of course, many of us in teaching don't mind offering sage advice over friendship issues or helping a student learn to do up a tie, but increasingly the changes seen in what is expected of schools have been remarkable. As noted in Chapter 4, these changes have been particularly marked since the Covid-19 pandemic, with staff reporting the need to support students as old as eight with toileting, needing to support students with sitting at a table and eating, and with dressing themselves, far beyond an age where one might expect able-bodied children to be able to do this independently.

Reflection: My Training Didn't Prepare Me for This

What's the most surprising or outrageous thing you've been asked to do as an educator for a child in your care? How did you respond?

Understandably, cries of 'it shouldn't be like this!' and 'it's not our responsibility!' abound, but getting lost in cycles of frustration is unhelpful and unproductive – it is what it is and we often have little choice but to respond to the immediate needs of the child in front of us with a trailing shoelace or an empty stomach – and the needs of communities during times of economic instability, division and fear...

When there's a mismatch between the expectations of parents, carers and communities and what a school's job is and that of the educators working there, all manner of problems can come into play. Parental complaints against schools are on the rise, with potentially catastrophic consequences for educators' careers, as noted in *Schools Week* in the UK in July 2024 (Dyson, 2024). In 2022–23, 1,684 reports were assessed by the misconduct unit at the Teaching Regulation Agency, more than double those seen in 2021–22 (Dyson, 2024).

According to the School Leaders Survey (Browne Jacobson, 2024), 68% say personal attacks and aggression towards staff are the most common types of negative behaviour experienced in schools. 70% of teachers believe parents and carers are now quicker to escalate concerns to a formal stage.

The impact of such complaints on staff wellbeing is catastrophic and is having a drastic effect on the quality of education schools are able to provide, as well as on retention, with calls for suicide prevention support for school leaders (Browne Jacobson, 2024).

WHAT'S GOING ON HERE?

I'd argue that there are two main things going on here. Firstly, schools represent authority within our communities. When the relationship works well, this means they offer sanctuaries of structure, safety and moral leadership. Unlike many other institutions in our communities there to keep us safe and functioning as communities, schools remained for the most part accessible during the Covid-19 pandemic. And whilst anxiety levels across our communities increased exponentially (see Chapter 4) and people couldn't access the doors of power in the form of government and policy-makers, community members could actually reach an actual human being in schools to vent their fear and frustration. On one level, it's a real honour to be perceived as the ones with all the answers ('I've given marriage guidance advice and even learned about her husband's STI,' said one headteacher), but on another, it's simply not realistic... And at worst, it means the senior leader, class teacher or support teacher becomes the scapegoat for all of society's ills.

The second factor that plays into this is that educators are, on the whole, remarkably practical and resourceful. So, whether it's an unexpected rodent in the classroom or the failure of the building's plumbing system, we're pretty darned good at finding a way through or around whatever is thrown at as. As a profession, we're 'do-ers' and will tend to get on with the task presented to us then save our questions over whether it's reasonable or not for later... then usually find that, later, we really don't have the energy... and so the cycle resumes.

This is all well and good when we are feeling positive and resilient and appreciated, but the rot sets in when we feel that our goodwill is being taken advantage of, as we pile exhausting new task onto unexpected new demand... and that's where the risk of burnout becomes very real.

THE IMPACT OF CHANGE

'You can't work in a school and not be good with change!' said a school leader I was coaching recently; and it's true that change is central to everything we do. But it's important to note that we each respond differently to it and, whilst this often provides richness and diversity in perspective and approach, it can also pose huge challenges within our educational communities.

Whilst many educators obviously thrive on the healthy challenge and infinite variety of a career in schools, and will relish spontaneity and the swift decisiveness required for an urgent decision, others will need time to process and robust and valid data and evidence to digest before they're likely to buy-in. And when people don't buy-in, whether it's through outright defiance or quiet resistance, things can quickly come crashing down.

Reflection: Perspectives on Change

How do you feel about change in general? Do you thrive on it and seek it out? Do you accept it and take a pragmatic approach? Do you need time to process information before you respond to it?

It's worth asking this question of your colleagues and those you manage – those who apparently 'resist change' aren't necessarily doing it to be difficult – they may simply need time to process and fully digest the information available. Those who might appear bitter or cynical are worth engaging with as they may have valid reasons for feeling this way and past experiences you can learn from together.

Whatever your instinctive reactions, it's worth acknowledging that change, whilst inevitable and often urgent, does have an impact on all in a school community. A change that might seem like a brilliant idea from a leader's point of view (having perhaps been to a conference and been blown away by a new model for behaviour management) might not be received with open arms at the chalkface.

When your school decides – or is compelled – to make a change or respond to external changes which have an impact on practice, it's always worth bearing in mind that this will have an impact on stakeholders in various ways.

Reflection: The Impact of Change

Regardless of your role, think about a change that you believe needs to happen in your school – this could be an adaptation of an existing policy, approach or routine, or an introduction of a new one. What impact is it likely to have in the following areas? Is this change likely to be perceived as positive, negative or neutral? What emotions might arise and how might you address these?

Staff – what is the likely impact on (and what are the implications for):

- Workload?
- Working conditions?
- Professional development?
- Job satisfaction?

Leaders – what is the likely impact on (and implications for):

- School culture?
- Strategic planning and operational delivery?
- Decision-making and communication?

Parents and carers – what is the likely impact on (and implications for):

- Communication?
- Relationships?
- School reputation in the community?

What other factors can you think of? Which other stakeholders might be affected?

Case Study: Managing Change – School Uniform Update

A newly appointed headteacher decided to update the school uniform, aiming for a version that was more cost-effective, durable, and reflective of the school's ethos. After conducting informal research and working with suppliers, the new uniform was announced to parents just two weeks before the summer holidays.

The change was intended to support families and modernise the school's image, but the response was mixed. Some parents appreciated the cost savings, while others were frustrated by the short notice – particularly those who had already purchased the old uniform. Staff also expressed concern about not being consulted and being unprepared to respond to parental queries.

In response to feedback, the headteacher introduced a phased rollout and opened communication channels with parents and students. The experience highlighted the importance of inclusive consultation, timely communication, and flexibility when implementing change in a school setting.

Reflection: Responding to Our Stakeholders

Consider three sets of parents and their response to the change in uniform:

Parent A welcomes the change and has no issue.

Parent B is initially resistant and then complies with the change.

Parent C struggles to meet the change.

How might they each respond to this change? What support do they need? What implications do their responses have for a) this policy, b) future policies?

CHANGE AND SCHOOL CULTURE

A review of the literature (see the references for further reading) in this area helps us understand how to nurture school cultures which are resilient and responsive to change and suggests the following characteristics are important:

1   **Shared vision and values:** Being explicit about and regularly revisiting and celebrating the values of your organisation will strengthen the school in its ability to navigate change effectively. The values compass activity in Chapter 1

is a valuable tool for exploring your individual and collective values as educators and exploring what these look like in practice in the classroom, corridors and meeting rooms.

2   **Openness to fresh perspectives:** Being receptive to innovation, new ideas and approaches is essential for adapting to change, alongside resilience and adaptability. This comes with a caveat that an eye for 'shiny, new things' is also risky, and that any innovation should be carefully planned and adapted with the needs of the students at the centre.

3   **A sustained focus on learning and development:** A commitment to continuous professional development ensures staff are equipped to meet the challenges of change. This should take into account the diversity of your community of educators and should ideally be bespoke, staff-led and tailored to the professional needs and priorities of each staff member and aligned to the goals of the organisation. See also **Collin and Smith's** report, *Effective professional development* (2021).

4   **Effective communication:** Well-planned, targeted, open and transparent communication with all those potentially affected by change builds trust and ensures everyone is appropriately informed. See also Dempster and Robbins (2017).

5   **Data- and research-driven decision-making:** The use of robust and relevant data is essential to inform decision-making and helps schools to make evidence-based changes. What constitutes 'valid' research is in itself a matter for debate, and examining a range of approaches and perspectives before deciding what's appropriate for your context is essential. See Hattie (2009) and Jones (2018).

6   **Empowerment of students and staff:** Fostering a culture that values the input and ideas of students and staff also fosters a sense of agency, ownership and engagement. See Hargreaves and Fullan (2002) and Biesta et al. (2015).

By cultivating these features, schools create an environment where change is not seen as a threat but as an opportunity for growth and improvement.

WHEELS: A MODEL FOR CHANGE

I'd like to end this chapter by proposing a simple, step-by step model for implementing change in schools, depicted in Figure 5.1. There are some brilliant models out there already, of course (see Kotter's model, 1996) and this obviously does not seek to usurp or replace them but combines some of the principles of my research in positive psychology, teacher identity and coaching practice to produce something that is both simple and adaptable for each unique context.

Figure 5.1   WHEELS: A Model for Change

Whether it's adjusting your own practice in the classroom, providing a tweak to the curriculum or responding to crisis or disaster, this model can help to break down and structure the process in a step-by-step manner. As we go through the model, consider how you might apply it to your context.

W: Who is involved in the change? Who will lead it? Who will be affected? What is the change you want to make? What will stakeholders be thinking, feeling and saying if the change is effective? What might get in the way and how will you overcome it? When does the change need to take place? What's the timescale and what check-in and evaluation points will you put in place? What might go wrong? It's worth doing a 'pre-mortem' or risk assessment of all the different hitches you anticipate and planning in advance what you might do to mitigate them.

H: How will the change be communicated? How will you remind those involved of the actions and how will you support them? How much time, money and resources will be needed and how have you budgeted for these?

E: What experience do you have of similar changes (whether the results were positive or negative)? What have you learned from these experiences? How will you ensure all who need to be are fully engaged with the changes?

E: What evidence are you drawing upon? How will you communicate this?

L: Who or what can help you leverage the change? What schools have done something similar and what can you learn from them? How will you foster and channel support at different levels of the organisation?

S: What's your strategy? Does this involve a written action plan? Who authors it, with whose input and who is accountable for the different elements? What systems will need to be reinforced, reviewed or introduced? How will you ensure the change is sustainable?

WHEELS: THE MODEL IN ACTION

Here's a worked example for how the WHEELS model could be applied to a change in the structure of the school day, including start and finish times.

W (Why, What, Who, When)

- **Why:** Clearly articulate the reasons for the change. This could include:
  - Improved student outcomes (e.g. better focus, increased engagement).
  - Enhanced teacher wellbeing (e.g. reduced burnout, better work–life balance).
  - Alignment with modern learning needs (e.g. later start times for adolescents).
  - Increased operational efficiency (e.g. staggered start/end times for traffic flow).
- **What:** Define the specific changes to the school day structure. This might include:
  - New start and finish times.
  - Adjusted break lengths and times.
  - Modified lesson block durations.
  - Potential for flexible learning time options.
- **Who:** Identify all stakeholders involved in the change process:
  - Teachers.
  - Students.
  - Parents/guardians.
  - School administrators.
  - Support staff.
  - Community members (if relevant).
- **When:** Establish a timeline for the change process, including:
  - Consultation and feedback phases.
  - Decision-making and planning stages.
  - Implementation and adjustment periods.

H (How? How Much?)

- **How:** Develop a detailed implementation plan outlining:
    o   Communication strategies to inform stakeholders.
    o   Training and support for staff.
    o   Adjustments to timetables and schedules.
    o   Logistics for transportation and before/after-school care.
    o   Evaluation methods to measure the impact of the changes.
- **How much:** Determine the resources required for the change, including:
    o   Budget for potential adjustments (e.g. transportation, staffing).
    o   Time allocation for planning and implementation.
    o   Staff training and development needs.

E Experience, Engagement

- **Experience:** Collect feedback from all stakeholders throughout the process to inform adjustments and improvements.
- **Engagement:** Foster a collaborative and inclusive approach, involving stakeholders in decision-making and change implementation.

E (Evidence, Evaluation)

- **Evidence:** Gather data on the current school day structure and any relevant research on optimal timing for learning and wellbeing.
- **Evaluation:** Develop a system to monitor and assess the impact of the new structure on:
    o   Student attendance, behaviour, and academic performance.
    o   Teacher morale and job satisfaction.
    o   Operational efficiency and resource utilisation.

L (Leverage)

- Identify opportunities to leverage existing resources and partnerships:
    o   Collaborate with other schools implementing similar changes.
    o   Utilise technology for communication and data management.
    o   Build on existing positive school culture and relationships.

S (Systems, Sustainability)

- **Systems:** Ensure the new school day structure aligns with overall school goals and policies.
- **Sustainability:** Develop strategies to maintain the new structure over time, including:

o   Ongoing evaluation and adjustment.

o   Communication and reinforcement of the benefits.

o   Addressing potential challenges and resistance.

CHANGE: THE GOOD, THE BAD AND THE INEVITABLE

Change is, paradoxically, a constant in education, and schools must adapt to remain relevant and effective. Ultimately, how it's perceived will come down to numerous factors and subjectivities and you know your communities best. Change can be refreshing and wonderful and invigorate the community by promoting innovation and improvement, modelling growth and resilience for our young people, sustaining a focus on professional development and improving community engagement. When it goes wrong, it can result in overwhelm, burnout, resistance and rebellion, be costly, literally and metaphorically, and it can risk exacerbating perceived or actual inequities and disparities in communities.

Reflection: Positively Embracing Change

Final reflections on you, your role and change:

- How can you foster a positive attitude towards change among your colleagues and students?
- What strategies can you use to manage your own workload and stress during times of change?
- How can you ensure that all students have the opportunity to benefit from change?
- What steps can you take to build strong relationships with colleagues, parents, and community members to navigate change effectively?
- How has your experience with change shaped your professional identity and goals?
- What collaborative approaches can be used to address the challenges and opportunities presented by change?
- How can you take on a leadership role in promoting positive change within your school community?

FOR LEADERS: SUPPORTING COLLEAGUES THROUGH CHANGE

1   **Understand the impact of change:** Recognise that change affects everyone differently. Some may thrive on it, while others may need time to process and adapt. It's essential to consider the possibility of diverse reactions and plan accordingly.

2   **Effective communication:** Clear, transparent, and timely communication is crucial when implementing change. This helps build trust and ensures that everyone is informed and on the same page.

3   **Involve stakeholders:** Engage all relevant stakeholders in the change process. This includes teachers, non-teaching staff, students, parents, and community members. Their input and feedback can provide valuable insights and foster a sense of ownership and collaboration.

4   **Leverage experience and evidence:** Draw on past experiences and relevant data to inform decision-making. Reflect on what has worked well and what hasn't, and use this knowledge to guide future changes.

5   **Support and empower your team**: Provide the necessary support and resources to help your team navigate change. This includes professional development, clear guidance, and creating an environment where staff feel valued and empowered.

WHAT WON'T CHANGE?

We've established how much can, will and does change, not just in a school term or year, but as any educator knows, in the space of seconds in the company of young people. As we conclude this chapter, I'd like to flip the concept on its head and consider what won't – or is unlikely – to change.

There will always be a need for education and educators – human beings naturally seek out others for guidance and cues as they develop into adults.

Children will always find ways of testing boundaries and resisting what might objectively be best for them (one of my recent favourites was a group of 14 year-olds insisting on wearing one white and one black sock each – there was nothing in the policy to say this wasn't allowed!).

There will never be a situation where we can brush our hands together and say, 'That's it! We're done. Let's keep it the way it is.' We will constantly need to evolve.

Back to my conversation with Pupé about preparing our children for a future we can barely begin to define: 'What *can* we do?,' I asked Karl. We pondered together for a while and eventually our conversation came full circle. Surely, we do what we do best. When we're exhausted and disillusioned, we throw our toys from the pram and are tempted to give up in despair. But when we're energised and optimistic, we *meet your young people where they are*, with curiosity, open minds and open hearts. We engage with them, we talk to then, we *ask them* what they need most. We place learning and growth at the centre of educators' professional development, encouraging them to look beyond the walls of their schools, conduct and share small-scale research projects and share these within, and ideally beyond, their schools. We insist they engage with the many rich dialogues happening around teaching and learning and signpost them to useful networks and powerful publications and research groups.

Rather than allowing a sense of hopelessness and ineptitude to breed, we do the opposite; we treat our educators as professionals. Because, ultimately, educators are, in fact, one of the few professions ultimately *not* to be under threat from AI. We know from the Covid-19 pandemic that neither students nor educators derived much joy from online teaching and learning and, whilst it has its place (e.g. for students who are unable to access school for exceptional reasons or if schools are forced to close temporarily), a diet of remote learning is highly unlikely to take hold.

And let's look down the mountain; look at what we've survived so far – our classrooms are still going, and many of us remain educators. There's still laugher, there are still lightbulb moments, we are still making a difference. It would be entirely understandable to be consumed by anxiety, but let's take Oliver Burkeman's perspective instead:

> *Most of what troubles us turns out to be tolerable, or even wonderful, or just never happens at all. Next time you worry that something's going to ruin your life, it's worth remembering that if you'd ever been right about that before, even once, your life would presently be ruined.* (2017)

Reflection: Looking Down the Mountain

Rewind your career back a year or so. Consider everything you were worried about at the beginning of the year. Was it as bad as you'd imagined? What unexpected challenges came about? Think about *how* you managed and what you can learn from it. Consider what skills and knowledge you have now that you didn't have then. What will you do with it next?

CONCLUSION

Navigating change in the education system is a complex yet essential task. Schools play a pivotal role in providing stability, security, and guidance amidst the turbulence of change. By fostering key skills and competencies in students, educators can prepare them for an unpredictable future. The WHEELS model offers a structured approach to implementing change effectively within schools. Embracing change with a positive attitude and collaborative efforts can lead to growth and improvement, ensuring that schools remain resilient and responsive to the evolving needs of their communities.

REFERENCES

Biesta, G., Priestley, M. and Robinson, S. (2015). 'The role of beliefs in teacher agency'. *Teachers and Teaching, 21*(6), 624–640.

Browne Jacobson (2024). *School leaders survey, spring 2024 – the results are in.* Browne Jacobson, 24 April. www.brownejacobson.com/insights/school-leaders-survey-spring-2024-the-results-are-in

Burkeman, O. (2017). 'Consumed by anxiety? Give it a day or two'. *The Guardian*, 15 September. www.theguardian.com/lifeandstyle/2017/sep/15/consumed-by-anxiety-give-it-day-or-two

Collin, J. and Smith, E. (2021). *Effective professional development*. Education Endowment Foundation.

Dempster, K. and Robbins, J. (2017). *How to build communication success in your school: A guide for school leaders*. Routledge.

Dyson, D. (2024). 'Teacher misconduct cases "driven up" by parental complaints'. *SchoolsWeek*, 30 July. https://schoolsweek.co.uk/teacher-misconduct-cases-driven-up-by-parent-complaints

Fullan, M. (2001). *Leading in a culture of change*. Jossey-Bass.

Hargreaves, A. and Fullan, M. (2002). *Leading professional learning: A guide to developing teacher agency*. Corwin Press.

Hattie, J. (2009). *Visible learning: A synthesis of over 800 meta-analyses related to achievement*. Routledge.

Jones, G. (2018). *Evidence-based school leadership and management: A practical guide*. SAGE.

Kotter, J. P. (1996). *Leading change*. Harvard Business School Press.

Organisation for Economic Co-operation and Development (OECD) (2024). *Future of education and skills 2030/2040*. October. www.oecd.org/en/about/projects/future-of-education-and-skills-2030.html

Warren Buffett Archive, Annual General Meeting (1992). https://buffett.cnbc.com/video/1994/04/25/buffett-you-dont-find-out-whos-been-swimming-naked-until-the-tide-goes-out.html?utm_source=chatgpt.com

Zahn, M. (27 March, 2024). 'AI could eliminate nearly 8 million jobs in UK, study shows'. ABC News. *https://abcnews.go.com/Business/ai-eliminate-8-million-jobs-uk-study-shows/story?id=108540016*

6

CAREER TRAJECTORIES
NAVIGATING THE HIGHS AND LOWS

This chapter explores:

- **Career trajectories**: Navigating the **highs** and **lows**.
- **Emotional highs and lows** in teaching.
- **Ambition** for **impact**.
- **Resilience** redefined.
- **Authenticity** and **self-awareness**.
- **Reflection** activities: Tracking and processing **emotions**.

THE EMOTIONS IN TEACHING

Teaching is an emotionally demanding job – the moods it evokes are varied, and ever-changing. As educators, we are, in my experience, masters of the 'swan' impression, where we appear to glide serenely on the surface, whilst grappling with a whole range of powerful emotions under the surface. As a wise coach called Sally once told me (when I returned her, 'So, how's Emma?' with the standard, 'Oh, fine… yep *fine*. I think…'), *all feelings matter* and are worthy of acknowledgement. One of the most powerful questions we can ask ourselves is, 'what is this feeling telling me?'.

For this next activity, I'd encourage you to consult Marc Brackett's table of emotions: https://marcbrackett.com/wp-content/uploads/2023/11/Mood_Meter_Marc_Brackett_Permission-to-Feel.pdf.

The four quadrants represent the levels of energy each emotion demands and how positive or negative they are likely to be for each of us. You might want to imagine it as a spectrum rather than four simple 'boxes'.

Reflection: Tracking your Emotions

Make a list of all the emotions you've felt in a given period – I'd suggest around 48 hours, but it will depend on your focus and priorities. You might want to ensure that the time period you choose includes a chunk of time in work. Don't overthink it.

Now start thinking about patterns. You may wish to colour-code the emotions, with red/pink representing high energy and negativity, yellow/orange representing high energy and positivity, blue representing low energy and negativity and green representing low energy and positivity.

What patterns do you notice? Does a particular quadrant dominate your list?

Lots of people in schools tend to find that their lists (as related to a school day or week) include lots of very high energy emotions and very few that are low energy but positive – how often in a school day do we feel 'serene' or 'chilled'?

Reflection: How Do These Emotions Feel?

Now focus in on three or four contrasting emotions on your list. Have a think about where in your body you experience the different emotions. If they had a texture or sensation, what might it be? If they had a colour, what might it be? You might want to compare them to an animal, a plant or another natural element. Excitement might be a light blue, gusty fluttering in the chest area; dread might be a murky green, slimy, squirming thing which you instinctively want to repel...

WHAT DO YOU DO WITH THESE EMOTIONS?

My experience again suggests that those of us working in schools and focusing on the needs of others are pretty adept at the 'keep calm and carry on' mantra, often pushing these emotions down and attempting to ignore them. With the negative emotions, this can result in the 'pressure pot' effect, where they eventually find a way of expelling their toxins – in my case, usually when I end up irritable with loved ones' over-perceived domestic crimes like leaving their muddy shoes strewn by the front door. With positive emotions, an inclination to modesty might lead us to take them for granted – your talents and actions might have led a considerable step forward for a young person but you dismiss it as 'just my job'.

Instead, what effective actions could you take to acknowledge, honour and learn from what these emotions are teaching you about your world?

For example, with negative emotions like stress or frustration, you might find cackling with a friend or colleague helps to process them, or a good old rant, tears in a safe space, just jotting down how you're feeling, or a good run or walk... With positive emotions, who do you share and celebrate these with? Again, journaling can be helpful, or structured spots in meetings for everyone to share a success from each working week, or a little box (virtual or physical) where you plonk all those little notes or emails of appreciation to pull out during a tough week.

Reflection: Processing Emotions

What helpful actions do you (or could you) take to process the emotions you regularly experience?

Here's a big coaching question. When you reach the end of your life, what do you hope to have achieved? How would you like people to remember you? What mark do you wish to have left on the world? What legacy do you wish to leave?

Reflection: You and Your Legacy

Write some notes or draw an image to represent the legacy you'd like to leave.

This question cuts right to the chase of what really matters. And, of course, what really matters will vary according to our individual circumstances and could look very different from the point of view of an ambitious 18-year old, a sleep-deprived parent, or a recently retired education professional.

Here's a slightly less terrifying angle to consider. What does 'career success' look like to you? You may wish to build on your reflections from Chapter 1. You can write or draw an image below.

Reflection: Career Success

Define your idea of career success using words or images.
How might this have looked different when you were 11 years old? Or at age 19?

Growth is central to human wellbeing; as human beings, we need to feel we are being stretched and challenged in healthy ways. A sense of forward momentum is arguably part of the human condition and is deeply ingrained in our language (where do you see yourself in five years? Where is your career heading?), the stories we tell ourselves and our perceptions of ourselves.

I often have the privilege of working with people at a metaphorical crossroads, making key decisions about their careers which are likely to have ripple effects that will affect the rest of their lives – to go for that promotion or not? To stay or leave their current context? 'But what if I make the wrong decision?' is a common worry. It can feel a bit like those *Choose Your Own Adventure* books (if you know, you know) – what if my decision takes me into the claws of the seven-headed monster? What if it results in my mangled body at the bottom of the canyon? This sounds flippant, but actually, those making such decisions have to, as responsible adults, consider potential career ruin, financial disaster, the loss of balance or happiness, when deciding which leap to take next. But ultimately, we always end up with this challenge: what if there is no 'right' or 'wrong' decision? What if you just do the best you can with the knowledge, resources and instincts that you have?

The idea that there's some hidden rule-book, some recipe for ultimate happiness and success to which others seem to have privileged access but which eludes us isn't uncommon, but the reality, in the words of a wise headteacher I know, is that we're actually all making it up as we go along – making the best of what we have with our experiences and our values as touchstones and guides.

This runs counter to the equally natural insistence that, if we reach the next goal, the next milestone, we will truly be happy. For many years, I believed that if I could just make middle leadership, then senior leadership, in my career, I would in some sense have found the holy grail, and would feel like a whole new, accomplished, polished version of myself. This belief was one that underpinned so many motivations and decisions through the early part of my career.

FORWARD MOMENTUM THAT FEELS RIGHT

The million-dollar question is how do we lean into the instinct for forward momentum in a way that feels right for us? How do we balance ambition with wellbeing, the desire to prove ourselves with self-belief, success with happiness? It's how we leverage the powerful yet often invisible frameworks for success which surround us whilst cultivating an awareness which is helpful and meaningful to us.

MY STORY

For the first 15 years of my career, I steadfastly climbed the ladder I saw before me. If you'd asked me if this is what I consciously set out to do, I'd have been utterly bemused, but I can mark out the rungs of the ladder with calls to my parents:

1998: 'Mum, dad, I've secured my first role' (as MFL teacher in a language college).

2003: 'Mum, dad, I'm head of department!'

2007: 'Mum, dad, I've made senior leadership!'

There were of course broken rungs and slippery rails along the way, but the moments of acceptance into these roles remain marked with a profound sense of pride and achievement. And I did thrive through those years, but it's easy with hindsight to forget the struggles that followed each transition – the definition and redefinition of my professional person, the sheer grappling of each new job description, the profound desire to earn the respect and esteem of my colleagues whilst feeling I was playing a game of whackamole.

Then, disaster! Or so it felt at the time. A senior leadership restructure. An internal application for the equivalent role to the one I'd already been doing. The 7 am sentimental walk around the school, where I dared to think of myself as part of the furniture after five years… and the disastrous interview, where I looked into the eyes of colleagues as familiar to me as my own family and floundered to articulate my 'impact'. The rejection, the sobbing on my colleague's dirty-blue polyester carpet. The humiliation of turning up the next morning again, puffy eyed, to face my colleagues again. The stroppy resignation that followed, and with it, the realisation that the 'ladder of success' was, frankly, a mirage.

Clearly, my career wasn't, as I'd imagined, destroyed, but this episode led to twists and turns, highs and lows, new disasters, and new adventures which I could never have anticipated.

From Ladders to Climbing Walls

So, if the ladder metaphor doesn't work, what does? Perhaps using a generational lens to consider this is helpful. Hannah Grady-Williams, CEO of D'Skills, in her keynote to international school leaders in Washington DC in 2025, offers a generational perspective to an audience of (predominantly) Gen-Xers. Young people these days, she said, view their careers more as a 'climbing wall'. This image is one we non-Gen-Xers could do with adopting – it's not vertical, it's in no way set out in advance, and this perspective allows us to broaden our perspective to seek growth and opportunity in areas beyond our immediate view.

AMBITION AND DRIVE – PURPOSE OVER EGO

In this section, we'll consider the tricky notion of ambition in teaching.

Ambition in teaching is often portrayed as climbing the ranks to leadership roles, but true ambition in education is about impact rather than status. How do we nurture a desire for meaningful change rather than career advancement for its own sake? It's important to consider the following:

- **Defining impact:** What does meaningful ambition look like in teaching? It may involve improving student outcomes, pioneering innovative practices, or mentoring colleagues.
- **Sustainable ambition:** Avoid burnout by aligning career goals with personal values.
- **Balancing drive and wellbeing:** How can teachers push themselves professionally while maintaining personal fulfilment?

As I type, I'm aware of two distinct responses to the idea of ambition in schools. First, there is the person who sets out on their teacher training with a clear goal to become, for example, a headteacher by the age of 30. Secondly, there is the teacher who will openly say, 'I'm just not ambitious. I'm perfectly happy in the classroom.' These two sketches are both problematic, and admittedly two-dimensional.

Ambition is an excellent thing – of course it is. When we see it ignite in the young people in our classrooms, we quite rightly celebrate and nurture this. In the world of education, there is a tendency to be wary of those who set out with a desire to move into leadership as quickly as they can. This view is one with which I have some sympathy – with decades in education, the stripes we earn are hard-won, often painful, and equip us to deal with painful, tricky and unpredictable situations with a wisdom and experience that is irreplaceable.

That said, great leaders come in many different forms, and I've been as positively influenced by young leaders as I have by more seasoned ones – fresh eyes and fresh perspectives also bring positive insights.

There's no 'right' or 'wrong' motivation for wanting to progress through roles, each one increasing in influence, in your career, but I would argue that keeping young people at the centre of those ambitions is key, and that self-awareness should be cultivated and healthy challenge embraced along the way.

Of course, ambition means far more than simply progressing to a 'higher' role (interesting how the language of roles in schools frequently defaults to relative height!), so let's think about the concept more broadly. Your ambition might be specifically related to a particular young person or class. It would be valid for it to be linked to test or exam results, but it might also be holistic – to encourage X to maintain eye contact when talking; for Y to pursue further study in your subject; to help develop a certain colleague in a particular way; to develop your knowledge and skills in a certain area.

Reflection: You and Your Ambitions

What are your ambitions:

- For the next term or semester?
- For the next academic year?
- For the next decade?

Think about your own professional development, your colleagues, your context, and be sure to keep your students (current or future) at the centre.

ROCKSTARS AND SUPERSTARS

Not everyone does or 'should' want to become a leader. In her book, *Radical Candor*, Kim Scott writes of two types of high-performing employees: '*rockstars and superstars*'. I've reflected below on how these two types of employees might show up in a school context.

> **Rockstars:** *Every school has its rockstars – the experienced, steady hands who bring consistency, deep expertise, and a calm, stabilising presence to their colleagues and students. These are the teachers and staff who keep things running smoothly, excelling in their craft and providing the foundation on which great schools are built.*

> **Superstars:** *Superstars, on the other hand, are the educators who are always looking for the next challenge – driven, ambitious, and eager to push boundaries. They thrive on innovation, leadership opportunities, and making change happen, often moving quickly up the career ladder.*
> (2019, pp.44–47)

As you read these descriptions, you may well be reflecting that there are times in your career when you've manifested – or are likely to manifest – both. I know in my mid-twenties, when I was working and playing as hard as I could, I would have given my left arm to be seen as a superstar, whereas when my kids were sleeping three or four broken hours each night, I was more than happy to be seen as a rockstar.

Here's a bit more about how these two types of (remember, both highly effective) colleagues might manifest themselves and how you might get the most out of them.

Rockstars in Schools

- The steady, experienced teachers who keep schools running smoothly – reliable, consistent, and utterly dependable.
- Subject and pastoral experts who take deep pride in their craft, bringing calm and stability to staff and students alike.
- The go-to colleagues for wisdom, support, and continuity, ensuring routines and systems remain effective.
- Skilled at sustaining high levels of productivity, managing classrooms with quiet confidence, and guiding students with steady expertise.
- Passionate about honing their specialisms – whether it's pedagogy, SEN support, or pastoral care – without the constant need for reinvention.

Superstars in Schools

- The ambitious, fast-moving educators who are always looking for the next challenge, whether it's leadership, curriculum innovation, or school improvement.
- Thrive on change, development, and taking on new initiatives to transform teaching and learning.
- The first to put their hands up for responsibility, keen to drive improvement, shape policy, and push for better outcomes.
- Natural innovators who bring fresh ideas, lead training, and challenge the status quo to improve education for students.
- Often seen as future school leaders, moving quickly up the career ladder with an insatiable drive to demonstrate impact.

FOR LEADERS: HOW TO GET THE BEST OUT OF ROCKSTARS

1 **Respect their expertise:** Recognise and celebrate their deep subject knowledge and classroom mastery. Give them opportunities to refine their specialisms rather than forcing them into leadership roles they don't want.

2 **Provide stability:** Rockstars value consistency, so avoid unnecessary upheaval. Instead, seek their input when introducing change to ensure smooth implementation.

3   **Encourage mentoring:** Their wealth of experience makes them invaluable as mentors to newer staff. Pair them with early career teachers or those looking to develop their classroom practice.

4   **Recognise their impact:** Leadership isn't the only measure of success. Ensure they feel valued for their contribution to the school's long-term success.

HOW TO GET THE BEST OUT OF SUPERSTARS

1   **Feed their ambition:** Give them meaningful leadership responsibilities, even before they step into formal leadership roles. Projects, initiatives, and opportunities to lead CPD can keep them engaged.

2   **Offer challenge and progression:** Superstars will seek new opportunities, so provide clear career pathways to retain them within your school. If they feel stuck, they may look elsewhere.

3   **Harness their energy wisely:** Their drive is an asset, but they need guidance to ensure their ideas align with the school's vision. Support them in developing strategic thinking.

4   **Balance enthusiasm with wellbeing:** Their eagerness to take on everything can lead to burnout. Encourage sustainable working habits and a focus on long-term impact rather than quick wins.

AVOIDING BEARTRAPS: 'SHOULDS', COMPARISON AND 'JUST'

The language of 'should's and 'shouldn't's can tie us up in all sorts of tricky knots. If a possible decision doesn't break the law, contravene safeguarding rules or do harm to you or anyone else, give yourself a break from such binds! Comparing yourself to others is also a big, unhelpful beartrap. Just because the person you graduated alongside is now an executive headteacher doesn't mean you need to strive to do the same.

These days, I'm a main scale teacher. I teach four different subjects and some-times deliver staff training. I caught myself, a couple of years ago, telling an old friend I was 'just' an English teacher. She gave me her very best Teacher Look. 'Would you let one of your coachees get away with that?' she asked, stern and disap-pointed. Ever since, I've called others up on this – you're never 'just' a teaching assistant, 'just' a member of office staff, 'just' a teacher. In fact, without our teaching assistance, our office staff, our site staff, our middle leaders, it would frankly all start to unravel. And our profession is essentially pyramid shaped – we literally need far more people at the chalk face than we do in leadership positions.

CHALLENGING THE STATUS QUO: MTPT AND NOW TEACH

Thank goodness for the brave and important voices who not only insist that it is possible to thrive as a parent and as an educator, but that it is imperative we insist on the conditions and reasonable adjustments which make it possible to do so. The Maternity Teacher/Paternity Teacher (MTPT) charity is doing some phenomenal work in terms of questioning old-fashioned assumptions and advocating for conditions that make teaching a sustainable career, including flexible working, networks and support with the transition into and out of parental leave. You can find a link to their website in the references.

Now Teach, an organisation with which I have proudly worked for the last seven years, also embraces the idea that we're likely to have more than one career before we retire, supporting successful professionals who are looking for a fresh challenge in the transition into teaching. The hundreds of teachers they've supported into the profession since 2017, with backgrounds from law, to nursing, to executive leadership, to aeronautical engineers, have breathed new life into our profession, bringing a level of wisdom and experience from which an increasing number of young people are benefitting. You can also find a link to their website in the references.

SQUIGGLY CAREERS, FLEXIBLE WORKING AND FRUIT-SALAD CAREERS

More and more educators are stepping away from the traditional 'ladder' of school leadership and embracing **squiggly careers**, what one inspirational coachee called **fruit salad careers**, and **flexible working** in ways that bring fresh energy and sustainability to their professional lives. Some are carving out portfolio careers, blending teaching with consultancy, coaching, writing, or research. Others are finding balance through part-time roles, job shares, or leadership positions that allow them to stay close to the classroom. The rigid, one-size-fits-all career path of the past is giving way to a more fluid, personalised approach – one that values individual strengths, wellbeing, and long-term retention over relentless progression. Schools that embrace this shift, offering creative career pathways and genuine flexibility, will reap the rewards of a workforce that is motivated, fulfilled, and in it for the long haul. Harley, an education researcher, reflects on the benefits and challenges of those who experience non-linear careers, challenging the dominant narrative of those who've been leaders stepping back 'down' into the classroom: 'Teaching is the heart of our profession, and we shouldn't feel uneasy about returning to it, no matter where our careers take us and yet some of the people I have asked were concerned about how some of their career choices would look to others' (Harley, 2025).

Here are two case studies from those who've forged their own unique paths and shared their 'squiggly careers'.

Case Study: A Squiggly Career in Uganda

Perspectives from Roles Alongside Teaching

I'm from Uganda. I wanted to share with you how my teaching career has taken a squiggly turn. I was always passionate about education. After running into problems during my career of being a Maths teacher, I expected to follow a traditional path – teach, gain experience, and move up the ranks. But things didn't quite work out that way. First, I found myself taking on a part-time gardening job to supplement my income. I know it sounds unrelated, but it actually helped me develop patience and a new appreciation for growth. Then, I started cleaning houses on the side to make ends meet. It wasn't glamorous, but it taught me the value of hard work and attention to detail. But the most unexpected turn was when I started working as a caregiver for a young boy. It was a role I never anticipated but gave me a profound sense of moral purpose and perspective.

Case Study: Nathan

Navigating Leadership and Teaching Challenges

For eight years, I served as the Deputy Head of a small co-ed day prep school, which had recently become part of an educational group. Following an Outstanding ISI report, the long-standing Head announced their retirement, and I applied for the position but was unsuccessful. Despite initial support from the new Head, my tenure took a sudden turn when I was given a term's notice without clear reasons.

The abrupt decision led to confusion and distress among staff and students. Despite positive appraisal documents and feedback, I was told to leave by Christmas. The Head and Education Director tried to persuade the company to let me stay longer, but the decision stood. The announcement caused a storm, with parents and staff expressing their anger and support.

Reflecting on the experience, I realised the impact of internal politics and the importance of mental health. The challenges continued as I transitioned to a new role in South-East Asia, facing the complexities of repatriation and a job search during the pandemic. Despite the difficulties, I found resilience and support from my family, ultimately returning to the UK and continuing my teaching career.

RECLAIMING RESILIENCE: A FRAMEWORK FOR GROWTH AND SUSTAINABLE SUCCESS

A coachee reflected back on her intial visit to a school before applying for a senior leadership role there. 'Not many people can hack it around here' a deputy head told her during this first encounter. The coachee reflected back on a subsequent academic year so challenging that it had led to significant weight loss due to missed meals, regular heart palpitations and a genuine threat to her closest relationships. 'I should have trusted my gut during that first visit – the signs were there in that comment from the deputy head!' Instead, flattered by the school's clear interest in her skills and experience and in need of a change following a bruising failed interview in her previous role, she determinedly accepted the role. It was only in November when she became aware that she wasn't seeing her own young children for days at a time (so early was she leaving the house and so late was she returning). It wasn't until January, when her closest friend staged an intervention, that she realised she'd stopped attending social events and become monosyllabic and stubborn (when previously she'd been chatty and ebullient) when asked how her work was going.

For too long, **resilience** in education has been mistaken for **endurance** – a badge of honour for those who push through exhaustion, overload, and impossible expectations. But true resilience isn't about survival; it's about growth, adaptability, and self-awareness. It's about knowing when to push forward, when to pause, and when to seek support. This model reframes resilience as a dynamic process, equipping educators to thrive, not just endure.

1 **Self-knowledge: Understanding your own strengths and needs**

- o Recognising your limits is not a weakness – it's wisdom.
- o Identify what energises you and what drains you.
- o Build self-reflection into your routine: What's working? What's not? What needs to change?

2 **Boundaries and sustainability: Protecting your energy**

- o Set and **stick to** clear work–life boundaries. Saying no can be an act of professional self-care.
- o Challenge toxic expectations that equate resilience with overwork.
- o Recognise that sustainable educators are effective educators.

3 **Growth through challenge: Learning, not just coping**

- o Reframe difficulties as opportunities for development – what can this teach me?
- o Develop a problem-solving mindset: What's within my control? What actions can I take?
- o Seek feedback and reflect without self-judgement – every challenge is a learning moment.

4 **Support networks: Strength in community**

- o Resilience isn't a solo endeavour – lean on trusted colleagues, mentors, and networks.

o   Foster a culture of open conversation where struggles can be shared without fear.

o   Prioritise relationships that uplift, inspire, and remind you why you came into this profession.

5   **Purpose and joy: Staying connected to your 'why'**

o   Keep sight of what drives you – whether it's making a difference to students, innovation, or collaboration.

o   Celebrate successes, no matter how small.

o   Infuse joy into your work – laughter, creativity, and moments of connection build long-term resilience.

Resilience isn't about **gritting your teeth and getting through it** – it's about **growing, adapting, and staying whole**. Let's reclaim resilience as something empowering, sustainable, and rooted in professional and personal wellbeing.

The bit that nobody tends to tell you as you embark on a career is that you're likely to learn far more about yourself during the challenging periods than the ones which feel like plain sailing. I know, for example, that I wouldn't be writing this book, or doing the work I do now, if it weren't for the stinging rejections, the disastrous oversights, the dangerous assumptions or the out-and-out tragedies I've experienced or witnessed over the last 26 years.

Reflection: Lessons from Experience

Draw a timeline in order to reflect back on your career. Draw a horizontal line to represent your career from the start to today. Put a cross and brief notes to mark three of your most rewarding experiences. Now do the same for your most difficult and adverse experiences.

Consider all six experiences – what did they teach you about:

- Your values?
- Your relationships?
- Your resilience?
- What you need in order to be most effective at work and at home?

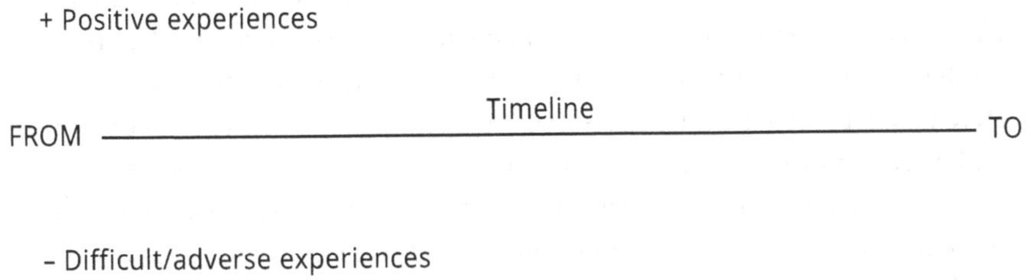

+ Positive experiences

Timeline

FROM ———————————————————————————— TO

− Difficult/adverse experiences

Figure 6.1   Timeline

LIMITING BELIEFS

If you're facing a setback, be it an unsuccessful job application or a loss of mojo that, now you come to think of it, has been going on for several weeks or months, it can be powerful to hold a mirror up to your beliefs about the world and about yourself. This isn't about beating yourself up for a mindset or attitude which is holding you back (oh, if only I were more assertive/confident/honest!). It's about recognising that your way of turning up in the world that has worked for you so far is no longer fit-for-purpose and could do with a tweak or a refresh.

Let's take two examples of limiting beliefs recently shared by educators:

'I must be busy/stressed all the time in order to be productive.'

'I don't have the right to feel bad because others have it worse.'

REFRAMING LIMITING BELIEFS

Let's apply the following key steps to the examples above:

1   **Recognise:** What is this belief and where does it come from?
2   **Reframe:** How could you see this differently?
3   **Release:** How does this belief no longer serve me? Why is now the time to release it?

Belief 1: 'I Must Be Busy/Stressed all the Time in Order to be Productive'

1   **Recognise:** This belief stems from societal pressures and cultural norms that equate busyness with success and productivity. It may be influenced by personal experiences or observations where hard work is celebrated, leading to the assumption that constant activity is necessary for achievement.
2   **Reframe:** Productivity can also be measured by the quality of work and the effectiveness of time management, not just the quantity of tasks completed. It's possible to be productive while maintaining a balanced and healthy lifestyle. Embracing downtime can enhance creativity and efficiency.
3   **Release:** This belief no longer serves me because it leads to burnout, anxiety, and a feeling of overwhelm. It's time to release it because recognising that rest and reflection are essential for sustained productivity allows for a more fulfilling and balanced life. Prioritising mental wellbeing improves overall performance and satisfaction.

Belief 2: 'I Don't Have the Right to Feel Bad Because Others Have it Worse'

1 **Recognise:** This belief often arises from empathy and the comparison of one's struggles to those of others. It may be rooted in a desire to minimise one's own pain in light of others' suffering, leading to feelings of guilt or inadequacy.

2 **Reframe:** Everyone experiences their own unique challenges, and it's valid to acknowledge personal feelings regardless of others' circumstances. Feeling bad is a human experience and recognising this can foster compassion and understanding both for oneself and for others.

3 **Release:** This belief no longer serves me because it invalidates my feelings and prevents me from addressing my own emotional needs. It's time to release it because embracing my emotions allows for healing and growth. Acknowledging my struggles is the first step toward resilience and self-compassion, which ultimately enhances my ability to support others as well.

By applying this framework, one can transform limiting beliefs into empowering perspectives that foster personal growth and wellbeing.

Reflection: Reframing Limiting Beliefs

Now identify a belief that has served you up to now but is no longer helpful to you and follow the same steps:

- Recognise.
- Reframe.
- Release.

HANDLING NEGATIVE FEEDBACK

'I have to be honest, Emma. I'm worried. I thought you were amazing but now I'm not sure.'

I'm sure we all have examples of negative feedback we've received, which really stung. This was after an observation with one of *those* bubbly Year 9 classes, where my ambitious plan and colour-coded worksheets just didn't land as I'd hoped. Some-one had smuggled a bag of sweets into the room. The boys had an ongoing game involving emitting animal noises and avoiding detection. I was flustered and not feeling 100%. Here is another that an educator shared with me:

'Your lesson just lacked pizzazz.'

The thing about teaching is that, whilst each country has a set of important, fundamental standards that must be met (for the sake of our young people), drop-in reviews and observations bring a whole new level of subjectivity. As a profession, we are fraught with targets and 'even better ifs' and it can feel we're utterly swamped in areas for improvement and, frankly, never quite good enough.

MANAGING NEGATIVE FEEDBACK AS A TEACHER (AND TRANSFORMING IT INTO GROWTH)

Teaching is an inherently personal vocation. You invest your heart, energy, and expertise into your students, so receiving negative feedback – be it from a colleague, a leader, a parent, or even a student – can feel quite disheartening. However, when approached thoughtfully, feedback can serve as a valuable catalyst for development rather than a blow to your confidence. Here's how to navigate it with resilience and purpose:

1 **Pause before reacting:** Whether it's an observation debrief, a complaint from a parent, or a comment from a student, take a moment to breathe before responding. Allow yourself the space to process the information without letting emotions take the lead.

2 **Separate yourself from the feedback:** Negative feedback does not equate to being a poor teacher. It pertains to a specific lesson, decision, or moment – not your entire career or self-worth.

3 **Look for the useful bits:** While not all feedback holds equal merit, there's often something to glean. Ask yourself: Is there a small, practical change I can implement that would enhance my teaching?

4 **Seek clarity if needed:** If the feedback feels vague or unhelpful, request specifics: 'Could you provide an example of what could be improved?' or 'What strategies would you suggest?' This can transform criticism into actionable steps.

5 **Recognise the source:** Consider who is delivering the feedback. Is it a trusted mentor or a frustrated parent? A constructive coach or a weary Year 9 student? Some voices will carry more weight – filter accordingly.

6 **Don't let it define you:** One challenging lesson or observation does not negate the myriad positive moments you create for your students. Maintain perspective – no one is perfect every lesson, every day.

7 **Reflect, adjust, and move forward:** If the feedback is valid, take it on board, adjust your approach, and move forward. Growth is an ongoing journey, and every teacher – regardless of experience – is still learning.

8   **Balance it with the positives:** Keep a 'feel-good folder' – emails from parents, kind words from students, and positive observations. When negative feedback stings, revisit these reminders of the impact you're making.

9   **Remember: Even the best teachers face criticism:** Teaching is a complex, emotional, and ever-evolving profession. If you're receiving feedback, it indicates that you're reflecting, improving, and evolving – and that's the hallmark of a great teacher.

By embracing feedback and adopting a growth mindset, you can transform challenges into opportunities for professional development and personal fulfilment.

BRINGING YOUR BEST, HONEST, AUTHENTIC SELF TO APPLICATIONS AND INTERVIEWS

Teaching is a profession rooted in relationships, passion, and authenticity. When applying for roles – be it a new teaching position, a leadership role, or a lateral move into something different – it's all too easy to fall into the trap of saying what you think interviewers want to hear. However, the best way to secure a role where you will truly thrive is to present your authentic self. Here's how to do it:

1   **Know your 'why':** Before you begin crafting your application or stepping into an interview, take a moment for reflection: Why do I teach? What impact do I wish to have? Schools seek educators who embody genuine passion and purpose.

2   **Be honest about your strengths:** Perfection is not a requirement. Embrace your strengths with confidence while also being open about areas where you seek growth. The best schools value reflective practitioners over polished automatons.

3   **Use real examples:** When discussing your skills, provide tangible examples. Instead of stating, 'I'm great at building relationships,' try sharing, 'Last year, I implemented a mentoring system for disengaged students, which led to improved attendance.' Authentic stories resonate more deeply.

4   **Don't just say what you think they want to hear:** Schools want to understand who you are, not merely hear you recite their latest Ofsted report. Be genuine in your responses; if a school's values don't align with yours, it may not be the right fit – and that's perfectly acceptable.

5   **Ask meaningful questions:** Remember, interviews are a two-way process. Inquire about the school's ethos, workload expectations, or initiatives for staff wellbeing. This demonstrates confidence, curiosity, and a commitment to finding the right environment for yourself.

6   **Let your passion shine:** Schools are on the lookout for teachers who genuinely love what they do. Don't shy away from expressing your

enthusiasm – whether that's a passion for your subject, a dedication to student wellbeing, or a desire to make a meaningful difference.

7 **Be yourself – the right school will recognise your value:** If a school fails to appreciate you for who you are, it's likely not the right place for you. The ideal role is one where you can be your authentic self while continuing to grow and flourish.

A teaching career is dynamic, full of highs and lows, and rarely follows a predictable path. By embracing a broader definition of success, fostering authentic ambition, and building resilience, teachers can navigate their careers with confidence and fulfilment. Each step, whether planned or unexpected, contributes to a rich and impactful journey.

CONCLUSION

In this chapter, we have explored the multifaceted nature of career trajectories in teaching, delving into the emotional highs and lows that educators experience. We discussed the importance of fostering ambition for impact rather than ego, and the value of redefining success on our own terms. The concept of 'squiggly careers' was introduced, challenging traditional hierarchies and encouraging flexible, portfolio careers. We also examined the significance of resilience, not as mere endurance, but as a dynamic process of growth and adaptability. Through case studies and reflections, we highlighted the diverse paths educators can take, emphasising the importance of authenticity, self-awareness, and maintaining a balance between ambition and wellbeing.

REFERENCES

Brackett, M (2023). *Mood Meter* https://marcbrackett.com/wp-content/uploads/2023/11/Mood_Meter_Marc_Brackett_Permission-to-Feel.pdf

Grady-Williams, H. (2025). 'Dear superintendent, what you need to know about my future'. AAIE Annual Conference, Washington DC, 4 February. https://app.glueup.com/event/aaie-59th-annual-global-leadership-conversation-116563/agenda-at-a-glance.html#agenda-at-a-glance

Harley, C. (2025) *Whose line is it anyway?*. 26 March. www.researchtoclassroom.com/post/whose-line-is-it-anyway-non-linear-careers-in-education

MTPT Project: The Maternity Teacher/Paternity Teacher Project. www.mtpt.org.uk

Now Teach. https://nowteach.org.uk

Scott, K. (2019). *Radical candor: How to get what you want by saying what you mean.* Pan Books.

7
FINDING THE JOY

This chapter explores:

- **Finding joy** in teaching despite the challenges.
- Celebrating **joyful moments** in the classroom.
- Experiencing **'flow'** in teaching.
- Practical tips for **cultivating joy**.
- The power of **humour**.

MY STORY

I've started at a new school. The weight and scope of my responsibilities are pretty daunting and I haven't even worked out how to use the photocopier yet. Amongst my responsibilities is to fast-track a group of linguists through their French qualification in a year. It's a mixed ability class which includes a couple of native speakers and at least a handful who haven't chosen to be there. But there's no backing out now, for any of us, so we roll up our sleeves and get on with the task in hand. Sussing out the range of individuals in front of me is the first task – finding out what motivates them, being curious about their lives and their quirks. Within weeks, we've established what could loosely be called a 'routine' of wildly competitive games involving fly swats and 'running (literally) dictation'; I've fielded questions about how close Creole is to the version of French we're learning, how many tenses exist in total, in the world, heard anecdotes about the child who thought he was buying a mini-receptacle when he ordered a 'baguette' and masterfully kept a straight face when teaching the word for the sea creature, the 'seal'. We ventured to Northern France for a sleep-deprived and enriching experience which saw students immersing themselves in market-shopping and meal preparation and reflecting on whether the sky at dusk looks different in France.

In what was otherwise a challenging year, I remember those lessons as an oasis – those periods of shutting the classroom door, focusing on the immediacy of what mattered and being utterly immersed in responding to the lapses in confidence, the frustrations and celebrating the lightbulb moments and wins. There was copious laughter. There were regular tears (occasionally my own). There was consistency, there was grit, there was determination, there was mutual support, and there was always optimism.

TEACHING AND THE POTENTIAL FOR JOY

This book hasn't flinched from examining many of the deeply difficult, challenging and painful elements of being an educator in the 2020s, but despite these, I do, and always will, argue that we are part of a profession with a huge capacity for joy, both in spontaneous moments and in a deeply lasting and profound form. This belief is reinforced by my encounters with thousands of educators every year. I often ask those who work in schools to articulate their 'why?' (see Chapter 1) and so many of the answers are infused with a sense of joy. This might be a fierce sense of purpose ('to make the world a better place'), or a sense of pride ('we get to do a really important job – the job which creates all other jobs'). Even more frequently, people respond with a simple: 'because it's fun!' Often, teachers speak of being able to channel their inner child: 'I get to be really daft, every day!', of just how *interesting* young people are, and, always, of friendships forged with colleagues over half-drunk cold coffees, shared disasters and bolstered resilience.

Returning to school after a holiday is always (yes, even after 26 years) associated with a wide range of emotions, from anxiety to optimism. The impostor syndrome invariably has a party around this time ('how do I remember how to do this? How did I ever do it?') and the sheer volume of information, updates and changes before the children step through the door can feel overwhelming. But once the children *do* enter the building, for the vast majority of us, the worries and complexities that dogged us drop away and we focus on the human beings presented in front of us. We embark on sharing our passion for our subjects, establishing secure spaces for learning and growth, responding to the needs of the learners in front of us and the sheer immediacy, unpredictability and urgency of this task is one we have the potential to – joyfully – lose ourselves in. Of course, it's not all roses – children press our buttons, push our boundaries and enter schools with a plethora of complex issues – but to be the adult in the room qualified, through graft, hard-won qualifications and experience, to help is truly, I would argue, a privilege – and a joy.

DEFINING JOY

Joy in teaching is the deep sense of fulfilment and satisfaction that comes from making a positive impact on students' lives, celebrating their successes, and finding moments of connection and growth, despite the inevitable challenges and stresses of the profession. It is about recognising and appreciating the small victories, the breakthroughs, and the meaningful interactions that make the hard work worthwhile.

This chapter isn't about toxic positivity – a pretence that everything is fine, all of the time, and if we just plaster on a smile, it'll be ok. Our systems are often far from perfect and the numerous, noisy, demanding, complex people can be both the best – and the worst – thing about our jobs. What this chapter does aim to do is offer you a chance – explicit permission, models and perspectives – to tilt towards the positive, the life-affirming, the silly, the funny elements of this complex profession. Because frankly, life is short and we deserve to be happy.

HIGHLIGHTING THE JOYFUL EMOTIONS

In schools, we all-too-often operate within a deficit model with loads of energy going into 'even better ifs' and development planning. Obviously, growth is essential and striving to be better is admirable, but this can be at the cost of celebrating our numerous successes and can ultimately lead to disillusionment. Building into meetings opportunities to capture 'wins' and inspirations, to counter the deficit model by sharing highlights of our week, is a great way of promoting a culture of joy.

Have another look at Marc Brackett's matrix of emotions: https://marcbrackett. com/wp-content/uploads/2023/11/Mood_Meter_Marc_Brackett_Permission-to-Feel. pdf. For this reflection, we're going to focus in on the *positive emotions*.

Reflection: Capturing and Savouring the Positive Emotions in Teaching

Make a note of all of the *positive* emotions you've experienced in a fixed period of time, say, the last 48 hours – feel free to mix home and school.
Take a moment to dwell in those moments and actively make a note of:

- What you could see.
- What you could hear.
- What you could feel (physically and emotionally).
- Anything you could smell.
- Anything you could taste.

Because as human beings we have a tendency to brush over the positive and dwell on the negative, this activity is helpful for restoring the balance.

BEING INTENTIONAL ABOUT HOW YOU'D *LIKE* TO FEEL

How do you *want* to feel at the end of a school week/day? Be mindful and intentional – reflect on activities and people most likely to invoke those emotions in you. If you'd like more serenity in your working life, find spaces in school where you're least likely to be disturbed (ideally not in a locked toilet cubicle, though many do resort to this). If you'd like more delight, heading over to your youngest students and hanging out in the sandpit or on the football pitch come highly recommended.

The aim of this isn't, of course, to experience exclusively positive emotions – that would, frankly, be impossible; and of course emotions are complex. Out of negative emotions, we can channel great positivity (e.g. if you're feeling frustrated, what's this telling you? What are your options?) We always have choices. If you're feeling angry, look back at your values compass and consider which of your values have been challenged.

ACTIVELY SEEKING OUT JOY

- Seek out your students outside the classroom and stop for a chat – discussions about animals are a sure-fire win. Once you know a student has a serious penchant for armadillos, you've got a hook that can last years!
- Consider how you process negative emotions – do you need to run it off at the end of the working day? Do you value turning the air blue with a trusted colleague in a soundproof room? Writing it down and literally putting it in a box (or the bin) can really help.
- How do you consciously treasure the positive ones – the moments of pride and fulfilment? If you get a compliment from a student or parent, make sure you keep it somewhere so you can come back to it later.
- Celebrate the wins – remember that we're in a difference-making business and that we invest in human capital. One teacher told me that if a student so much as thanks her for a lesson, she literally gives herself a high five. We are notoriously rubbish at this as a profession and will often shrug off significant achievements as 'it's just my job', but taking time to recognise and value the difference we make is essential.
- Be proud! You're up at the crack of dawn, fighting the good fight, as a much-loved headteacher used to say – you're at the chalkface, tying the shoelaces, refereeing the disputes, asking the questions and modelling how adulthood looks.
- Treasure the fun – when I ask people why they do the job they do, aside from many references to moral purpose and difference-making, I often get the response that 'it's fun'. And, despite the challenges, we get to work with the most gloriously unpredictable, authentic, honest, funny beings – let's celebrate this!
- Laugh often and heartily – the power of humour is immense and we'll explore this later in the chapter.

LIGHTENING UP

I was terribly serious about my profession for many, many years. I took setbacks and defeats very much to heart and allowed them to dent my sense of self-worth, whilst also seeing praise and progression as validation of my worth as a human being. My husband (a journalist) and I would argue fiercely and passionately about whose job was more important – more demanding, more tiring, more worthwhile.

I remember embarking on a hugely ambitious class project (involving numerous colour-coded worksheets, a complex points system and hours and hours of onerous planning, sticking and folding). It went catastrophically wrong very early on, but I determinedly persisted. There were many, many snotty tears in the office until my head of department said, 'Leave it! Do something else instead.' This rather obvious-sounding solution provided a lightbulb moment for me at the time and I revisit it often.

Our job is important, our job is essential, but it's worth remembering we're not literally fighting fires, landing planes or operating on hearts and that if things go awry, which they so often do, there is nearly always another way forward – that every lesson, every day, every week is a fresh start. Children more often than not remind us of this daily – the child whose struggles or defiance gave you a sleepless night will more often than not surprise you with a cheery 'morning, Miss' the following morning, making you wonder why on earth you wasted those hours fretting.

Chödrön's *When Things Fall Apart* provides some powerful perspectives to help us take ourselves a little less seriously. She comments that, 'The most difficult times for many of us are the ones we give ourselves' (Chödrön, 1997, p.33) and these lines, I suspect, will strike a chord with educators! She goes on to suggest that 'maybe the most important teaching is to lighten up and relax' (Chödrön, 1997, p.181). Sometimes, taking ourselves a little less seriously is just the shift in perspective we need.

For more on dealing with negative feedback, see Chapter 6.

BLOCKING OUT THE NOISE OF CRITICISM AND JUDGEMENT

Almost everyone has been to school and almost everyone has an opinion about how schools should function. The endless pursuit of a silver bullet to solve the problems in our schools rumbles on on social media, frequently descending into hostility and some staggering displays of unkindness and lack of professionalism. Binary oppositions and oversimplifications of 'trauma informed' education vs 'zero tolerance' approaches, of 'progs' and 'trads' have persisted as long as the social media platforms have given them oxygen and have been exacerbated by the pesky algorithms that capitalise on the human negativity bias and know that negativity gains more attention, time and clicks than positivity. Again, I have made the mistake of allowing myself to get drawn into this, to get wound up, to invest personally in such debates and have learned the hard way that it's simply not worth my emotional energy.

Put in place healthy boundaries to insulate yourself from the unhelpful cacophony, in the knowledge that you're getting on with it, in your own way; you're 'in the arena', as Brené Brown puts it:

> *If you are not in the arena getting your ass kicked on occasion, I am not interested in or open to your feedback. There are a million cheap seats in the world today filled with people who will never be brave with their own lives, but will spend every ounce of energy they have hurling advice and judgement at those of us trying to dare greatly. Their only contributions are criticism, cynicism, and fear-mongering. If you're criticizing from a place where you're not also putting yourself on the line, I'm not interested in your feedback.* (Brown, 2012, p.20)

LAUGHTER AND HUMOUR

In the following section, we'll explore one of my absolute favourite subjects – the power and importance of laughter and humour in schools.

Reflection: Laughter in Schools

When did you last laugh with your students? Take a moment to dwell on the moment. What happened? What was the impact?

Firstly, let me share some powerful statistics I came across recently.

Research from the University of Kentucky (Whipple, 2008) suggests that children laugh around 300 times a day. I was quite staggered by this figure, which I came across during the summer holiday, whilst away with my teenagers and four of their friends, so I tuned in. From giggles to guffaws, it was almost constant. Opportunities for silliness, self-deprecation, taking the mick out of one another were rarely passed over.

And what about adults? The average, according to the same piece of research, is just 17 times a day. Whilst the gap is a little worrying on one level, isn't it glorious that we get to work with people who laugh so much? Laughter helps build all-important trust and rapport with young people.

Reflection: Conscious Building in Humour

Over the next working week, take a moment to make a note of the things that make you laugh, within the classroom and beyond. How can you maximise them in the future? Set yourself a goal of 20 or 30 laughs a day and see how you get on. Take note of the impact on your wellbeing.

Our sense of humour is pretty unique to each of us and it's very important to be sensitive to this, as well as always observing the required standards of professionalism and mutual respect. Bearing this in mind, let's have a look at five types of humour that we might come across in schools.

1. Affiliative Humour

This type of humour is used to enhance relationships and create a positive atmosphere. It involves telling jokes and funny stories that everyone can enjoy.

Example: A colleague shares a funny story about their pet's antics during a staff meeting.

Benefits:

- Enhances team cohesion and camaraderie.
- Reduces stress and creates a more enjoyable work environment.

Setbacks:

- May not be appreciated by everyone, especially if the humour is not inclusive.
- May be perceived as time-wasting or distracting, especially if there are time pressures.

2. Self-Enhancing Humour

This involves maintaining a humorous perspective on life, even in the face of stress or adversity. It's about finding humour in one's own situation.

Example: A class is particularly lively. The teacher says: 'Well, if teaching doesn't work out, at least I'll have a backup career as a referee.'

Benefits:

- Helps individuals cope with stress and maintain a positive outlook.
- Can inspire resilience and a sense of control over challenging situations.

Setbacks:

- If overused, it might come across as unprofessional or as not taking one's role seriously enough.

3. Aggressive Humour/Sarcasm

This type of humour can be used to criticise or mock behaviours and situations that might feel silly or unreasonable, often in a sarcastic manner. It can sometimes be used to assert control or express discontent.

Example: A teacher sarcastically comments, 'Oh great, another data collection. This will truly enhance the lives of our learners.'

Benefits:

- Can be a way to express frustration or question unreasonable systems, procedures and behaviours.
- Might bond individuals who share the same sense of humour.

Setbacks:

- Can create a hostile or uncomfortable environment if not used carefully.
- May be perceived as bullying or disrespectful.

4. Self-Defeating Humour

This involves making oneself the butt of the joke, often to create a sense of humility, gain approval or avoid conflict.

Example: A colleague jokes about their own forgetfulness, saying, 'I'm so flipping useless. I don't know how I function as an adult.'

Benefits:

- Can make the individual seem more approachable and humble.
- May diffuse tension and make others feel more comfortable.

Setbacks:

- Can lower the individual's self-esteem over time.
- Might encourage others to view the individual as less competent.

5. Dark Humour

This type of humour involves making light of subjects that are generally considered serious or taboo. It can be a coping mechanism for dealing with difficult situations.

Example: A colleague jokes about a particularly challenging day and says: 'At least nobody died.'

Benefits:

- Can provide a way to cope with stress and difficult situations.
- Might help to normalise and discuss challenging topics in a less threatening way, bonding those involved.

Setbacks:

- Can be offensive or inappropriate if not used sensitively.
- May alienate those who do not share the same sense of humour.

Reflection for Leaders: Humour in Your School

What type of humour is most common in your school or team? How can you foster laughter whilst ensuring it's as inclusive as possible?

JOY AND FLOW

If we're thriving in our work, we're likely to regularly achieve a state of flow. Mihaly Csikszentmihalyi describes 'flow' as a state in which 'people become so involved in what they are doing that the activity becomes spontaneous, almost automatic; they stop being aware of themselves as separate from the actions they are performing' (Csikszentmihalyi, 1990, p.53). Flow is an active (as opposed to a passive) state and requires conscious effort, but the results include exhilaration and fulfilment: 'One of the most frequently mentioned dimensions of the flow experience is that, while it lasts, one is able to forget all the unpleasant aspects of life' (Csikszentmihalyi, 1990, p.58).

To gain 'flow' in the classroom can take a bit of time but it's well worth staying attuned to the feeling, even if it's fleeting, for example in an interaction with an individual child or when engrossed in sharing a concept or idea you're passionate about with young people or colleagues. I'd say it was about three years into my teaching career before I consistently experienced it, but recognising it was when I truly realised I'd chosen the right career for me.

Whilst the noisiness and messiness of working in schools is acknowledged, I'd argue that the act of educating young people offers numerous opportunities to experience 'flow' and it's worth actively examining different ways in which this might be sought and achieved, as it's closely associated with joy.

Flow requires appropriate levels of skill and challenge, as illustrated by the image below. Where skill levels are high but challenge is low, educators are likely to feel relaxed (rather than actively stimulated); where challenge is high and skill levels are low, they're likely to feel anxious. Where skill levels are high and so are levels of challenge, flow is possible.

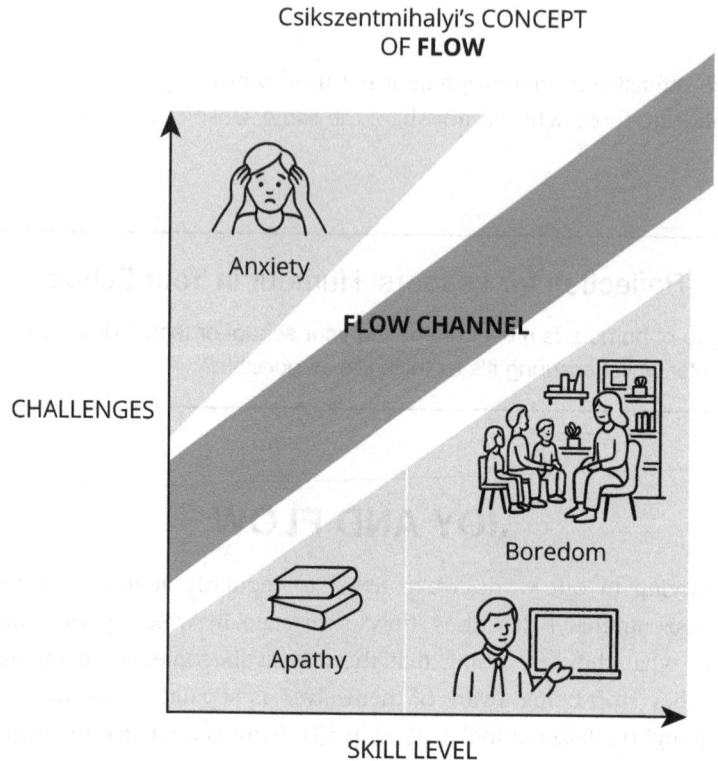

Figure 7.1 Flow for Educators

Source: https://chatgpt.com/ (15 April 2026)

Let's have a look in more depth at the stages of flow, with examples of how these might apply to educators.

Joy and Flow: Stages and Examples for Educators

1. Challenge-Skills Balance

Description: Flow requires an equal balance between the skill level and the challenge. If the challenge is too demanding, we get frustrated. If it is too easy, we get bored. In a flow experience, we feel engaged by the challenge, but not over-whelmed.

Example: A teacher designing a new curriculum finds the task challenging yet manageable, using their expertise to create engaging lessons without feeling stressed.

2. Action-Awareness Merging

Description: We are often aware of and thinking about something that has happened, or might happen, in another time or place. But in flow, we are completely absorbed in the task at hand.

Example: Whilst marking books, a colleague becomes so absorbed in the progress their students have made and in providing constructive feedback that they lose track of time and are fully present in the moment.

3. Clear Goals

Description: In many everyday situations, there are contradictory demands and it is sometimes quite unclear where we should focus our attention. However, in a flow experience, we have a clear purpose and good grasp of what to do next.

Example: A teacher sets a clear objective for a professional development session, such as 'Learn three new strategies for meeting the needs of neurodiverse individuals in your classroom', providing a focused direction for their learning and, most importantly, a clear focus on the needs of the students – a driving, guiding motivator for all educators.

4. Unambiguous Feedback

Description: Direct and immediate feedback is continuously present so that we are able to constantly adjust our reactions to meet the current demands. When we are in flow, we know how well we are doing, all the time.

Example: During a lesson, a teacher receives immediate feedback from student engagement and participation, allowing them to adjust their teaching methods on the spot. Or feedback from a line manager is focused and specific enough to leave the teacher feeling empowered about next steps.

5. Concentration on the Task at Hand

Description: High levels of concentration narrows our attention excluding any unnecessary distractions. Because we are absorbed in the activity, we are only aware of what is relevant to the task at hand, and we do not think about unrelated things.

Example: A teacher preparing for a class is so focused on creating interactive activities that they are not distracted by emails or other tasks.

6. Sense of Control

Description: An absolute sense of personal control exists, as if we are able to do anything we want to do.

Example: A colleague leading a workshop feels confident and in control of the session, effectively managing time and engaging participants.

7. Loss of Self-Consciousness

Description: A lack of awareness of bodily needs as self-consciousness disappears. We often spend a lot of mental energy monitoring how we appear to others. In a flow state, we are too involved in the activity to care about protecting our ego.

Example: While delivering a topic they are passionate about, a teacher is so immersed in the subject matter that they forget about their own self-consciousness and focus entirely on the content and student responses.

8. Transformation of Time

Description: A distorted sense of time occurs. Time either slows down or flies by when we are completely engaged in the moment.

Example: A colleague working on a creative project for their classroom realises that hours have passed without them noticing because they were so engaged in the task.

9. Autotelic Experience

Description: Flow is an intrinsically rewarding activity; the activity becomes autotelic, an end in itself, done for its own sake.

Example: A teacher who loves teaching finds joy in the act of teaching itself, feeling fulfilled and energised by the experience.

Reflection: Tracking Flow

Track your working day or week. Make a note of the moments when you experience any of the stages of flow described above. Take a moment to dwell on and savour the moment.

What was happening? Consider the five senses. What factors helped you block out unhelpful interference and 'noise' and truly exist in the moment?

What might you tweak or bring under your control to allow you to experience more frequent states of flow? You might try, for example, putting you devices on 'airplane mode' when you want to fully concentrate or actively seeking out quieter spaces in school (where possible) where others are less likely to be able to find you. Simply taking yourself away from adults and into the presence of children, whether it's dropping into a lesson or joining them in the sandpit, can be a great way to engineer flow.

ATTENTION MANAGEMENT

Finding time to focus – really focus – on a task during a working day in school can be really, really challenging, because schools are hotbeds of last-minute interruptions to interrupt your trains of thought. These could be from an enthusiastic colleague wanting to discuss their next lesson, a child wanting to show you their work or a sudden, ominous roar from the playground. Welcome or unwelcome, regular interruptions can mean you having to lug a load of work home with you, which is rarely good for the soul. Here are five tips for keeping us much of your workload as possible within reasonable hours – and getting it done whilst in the building, if that's what you'd prefer:

1   Try the Pomodoro technique (Cirillo, 2025). It's simple but effective – 25 minutes of focused work followed by a 5-minute break. It helps create a sense of urgency and keeps you moving forward. Pop a timer on, let those around you know you're having a 'head down' moment, and reward yourself with a cuppa at the end.

2   Find your quiet space. Whether it's a corner of the staffroom, an empty classroom, or even the library, having a go-to spot where you can breathe and think makes all the difference. Don't be afraid to claim a little pocket of calm in the chaos.

3   Noise-cancelling headphones can be a game-changer. Not only do they block out distractions, but they also send a gentle message to others that you're in the zone. A bit of instrumental music or white noise can help you tune in and shut the rest out.

4   Protect your planning time like gold dust. Block out short, specific windows in your day and make it known that this is your focused work time. A polite sign on the door or a quick heads-up to colleagues can work wonders. It's not about being unapproachable – it's about surviving the day with some sanity intact.

5   Batch the little things. Instead of reacting to every small interruption, keep a notepad handy and jot things down to deal with later. A quick sweep of the little jobs at the end of the day can stop your focus from being chipped away bit by bit all day long.

PERSPECTIVE AND THE NEGATIVITY BIAS

As I'm writing this chapter, a particularly shocking and gruesome news story is unfolding in my local area and I have found my attention drawn away from my writing no fewer than five times in the last hour to delve for updates. Consciously, I want to be focusing on this book but my unconscious mind is drawn repeatedly to the negative... I am reminding myself the negativity bias is inherently human and entirely natural – as human beings, we're wired to survive, not to be happy... As Dr Rick Hanson explains to Adrian Bethune:

> Our ancestors as they evolved needed to both avoid sticks [...] like predators and get carrots [...] like food. But the difference is this: If you fail to get a carrot today, you're going to get a chance to get one tomorrow. But if you fail to avoid the stick today, WHACK. No more carrots. (Bethune, 2020)

Countering the negativity bias is not about making big, dramatic changes but about gentle tilting towards the positive – about celebrating and capturing the wins, however small.

If we imagine a see-saw, it's about taking small, decisive actions to tip it to the positive, such as Martin Seligman et al.'s 'three good things' (Seligman et al., 2005; see Bethune and Kell 2020, p. 17 for an overview of how to use this in your role and life).

Taking a moment at the end of each day to note down 'three good things' in a notebook is a great way of training yourself to focus on the positive – and to resist the temptation to instead end your day with a quick check of your work email or a last look at the news headlines.

Deb Dana (2024) shares the concept of 'glimmers', 'tiny sparks' of feeling 'safe enough or ok enough in the world'; the moments that bring joy or connection (in contrast to triggers). This is also a powerful and non-threatening tool for fostering positivity. Glimmers are not about toxic positivity, she emphasises, but about noting the lighter, positive moments as they land in our systems and allow us to feel fully present in our lives.

FOR LEADERS: CAPTURING THE HIGHLIGHTS

Try starting meetings with 'highlights' or 'sparks' of the week. This doesn't take long at all but should encourage everyone (alone, in pairs or as a group) to note something that's gone really well for them – a breakthrough with a student, a moment of kindness or generosity from another person or a sense of accomplishment.

A LABOUR OF LOVE

When I speak to educators about their work, beyond the narratives of toxicity and overwhelm, there is so often talk of love. Love for a subject, love for the variety and unpredictability, love for the sense of human connection and doing something that really, really matters. Even those who've left the classroom, bitterly or reluctantly, will often speak of having 'loved' their time with the children but having found the rest of the job unsustainable.

When we educate, we have innumerable opportunities for curiosity, surprise, wonder and enchantment and it can truly feel, in the words of Sir John Jones, that we are in the business of weaving magic (2011).

Sir John makes the simple and powerful link between wellbeing and effectiveness in a talk in 2013: 'We are far better and more effective as humans when we're in a good mood'. In this powerful talk, he reminds us of what a unique privilege it is to be a teacher, citing George Steiner:

> The calling of the teacher. There is no craft more privileged. To awaken in another human being powers, dreams beyond one's own; to induce in others a love for that which one loves; to make of one's inward present their future; that is a threefold adventure like no other. (Steiner, 2003, p.183–184)

HANG ON TIGHT AND ENJOY IT: EMBRACING THE UNPREDICTABILITY

Let's face it, working in a school is a veritable roller coaster. If it's making you feel vomitous and giving you a headache, you always have the chance to go off and do something else instead. But if you choose to stay, why not embrace the unpredictability, hold on tight, and enjoy the ride?

Rather than feeling like victims of currents beyond our power, let's remember that, as autonomous adults with qualifications and skills, we always have choices, and reframe our obligations as choices. We get to be resourceful, creative, imaginative. We get to learn more about human behaviour than in almost any other profession. We get to say we're making a difference.

MOMENTS OF JOY: EXAMPLES FROM THE CHALKFACE

Rather than extended case studies, to end this chapter, I've taken snippets from examples of joy in the classroom. As with all contributions, these have been anonymised.

You and Your Legacy

- Bumping into an ex-student and hearing them reminisce about their best memories of being in my class – moments I had forgotten. Makes it all worth it.
- A student making their way over whilst I was enjoying a Saturday morning coffee to remind me that I'd taught them in Year 6 and tell me they were expecting their first baby.
- An ex-student getting in touch on social media to tell me how I'd inspired their love of, and pursuit of, my subject.
- Finding out an ex-student has just become a Geography teacher too! She sent me a message on 'Thank a Teacher' day to say thank you for my impact on her. What a privilege to be part of her journey.
- That moment when someone tells you you inspired them to believe in themselves and that your impact has stayed with them.

The Power of Noticing and Inclusion

- As a teaching assistant, I noticed a student regularly being 'vacant' in class. Other staff put it down to disengagement, but I kept pushing. Eventually he was diagnosed with epilepsy – his mum still thanks me!
- Hosting our school's first Iftar. A parent came and showed me a photo of herself at our school and said she'd never have imagined a time when the

school would celebrate alongside her. Makes me emotional every time I think of it.

- Newly arrived child from Africa via Germany. It started to snow. She'd never seen snow before. The whole class headed outside to share the moment of wonder with her.
- I'm autistic. I had a moment of feeling really overstimulated in the classroom. A student noticed and said, 'Are you autistic too, Miss? That's how it is for us sometimes, isn't it?' We had a chat about it later. The joy of validation.
- 'Thank you, Sir. You were the first teacher who made me realise I wasn't thick.' This was a severely dyslexic student who came to thank me when he achieved a Level 5 in Science at the end of primary school.

The Support of Colleagues

- My manager observed my lesson. Afterwards, he said, 'I spent the whole lesson wishing you had been my teacher.'
- I had an emergency at home, which sent me into a panic. My teaching assistant, who I didn't know well, got me a glass of water and said, calmly and firmly, 'Just go. I'll deal with everything from here.' I'll never forget her kindness and reassurance.

Magic and Hilarious Moments in the Classroom

- Reading *Private Peaceful* in the classroom with the light dimmed. A few muffled sobs as we came to the end – otherwise silence. The simple power of reading together.
- An 11-year-old student pointed out that my slide said 'self-asses' rather than 'self-assess'. Cue: uncontrollable giggling.
- Using the term 'naked eye' in a Year 4 Science lesson on microscopes. 'Naked, Miss? NAKED??' I completely lost the class to uncontrollable laughter.
- A PSHE lesson discussed consent and nudity. I mentioned the London naked bike ride. Incredulity from the class. One student said: 'I wouldn't have thought that would work. Less ding ding, more flop flop flop…'

The Positive Impact of Children on our Mood

- I was struggling to hide my stress and exhaustion one week. A student emailed me at my school email address to check I wasn't putting on my 'everything is fine' mask – a concept we'd discussed in tutor time when talking about mental health. My students regularly offer me much-needed kindness and perspective.
- Dragging myself into work during a series of personal challenges. My students always find a way of making me laugh – being with them is such a tonic!

Your Impact on Families

- Telling a mum what a great job she'd done to raise such a thoughtful and kind child and seeing tears well up in her eyes.
- Hard-working parents scared for their child's future. He made it to the Brit School and has since starred in a major West End show. I hope they're half as proud as I am!

CONCLUSION

Let us remember that the essence of teaching lies not just in the transmission of knowledge, but in the joy and fulfilment that comes from those magical moments of connection and growth. Despite the myriad challenges and pressures that educators face, it is the laughter, the lightbulb moments, and the shared triumphs that make this profession truly special. Embrace the unpredictability, cherish the small victories, and never lose sight of the profound impact you have on the lives of your students. Teaching is not just a job; it is a labour of love, a journey of discovery, and a celebration of the human spirit. Let us continue to find joy in our work, for it is this joy that sustains us and makes our efforts worthwhile.

REFERENCES

Bethune, A. (24 August 2020). *'Vlog with Dr Rick Hanson'*. www.teachappy.co.uk/post/teachappy-vlog-dr-rick-hanson

Bethune, A. and Kell, E. (2020). *A little guide for teachers: Teacher wellbeing and self-care*. Sage.

Brackett, M. (2023). *Mood Meter* https://marcbrackett.com/wp-content/uploads/2023/11/Mood_Meter_Marc_Brackett_Permission-to-Feel.pdf

Brown, B. (2012). *Daring greatly: How the courage to be vulnerable transforms the way we live, love, parent, and lead*. Penguin,

Chödrön, P. (1997). *When things fall apart: heart advice for difficult times*. Shambhala.

Csikszentmihalyi, M. (1990). *Flow: The psychology of optimum experience*. Harper Collins.

Cirillo, F. (2025). The Pomodoro technique. www.pomodorotechnique.com

Dana, D. (2024). 'Deb Dana on glimmers'. Norton Mental Health, 22 August. www.youtube.com/watch?v=WPwp6nyotME

Jones, J. (2011). *The magic weaving business: Finding the heart of learning and teaching*. Leannta Publishing.

Jones, J. (2013). BRAES. www.youtube.com/watch?v=VYYnge3mWhs&t=103s

Seligman, M. E. P., Steen, T. A., Park, N. and Peterson, C. (2005). 'Positive psychology progress: Empirical validation of interventions'. *American Psychologist*, 60(5), 410–421. DOI: 10.1037/0003-066X.60.5.410

Steiner, G. (2003). *Lessons of the masters*. Harvard University Press.

Whipple, C. (2008). 'Connecting laughter, humour and good health'. University of Kentucky, College of Agriculture, Food and Environment. https://fcs-hes.ca.uky.edu/sites/fcs-hes.ca.uky.edu/files/hsw-caw-807_0.pdf

8

LIFE HAPPENS

This chapter explores:

- **The role of your job** in your identity and the impact of life events.
- **Life events** affecting perceptions of professional roles.
- **Supporting** ourselves and others during life changes.
- **Planning** and having clear policies for unexpected events.
- **Reflections** on **life events** and their link to professional wellbeing and effectiveness.

WORKING WITH HUMAN BEINGS IS MESSY: THE IMPORTANCE OF PLANNING

In the education system, a high priority is given to planning, from that of individual lessons, sequences of learning or whole school development priorities. Although I admit that, for many years, I found such activities tedious and rather boring, as I've matured in the world of education, I completely appreciate their vital importance. It's in the 'cracks' – where misunderstanding and ambiguity is possible – that the problems appear. 'My colleague was allowed three days off for her son's graduation and I only get a day, unpaid?' 'How come she's allowed to come in late on a Tuesday and I'm not?' 'What do I do if I get a call and a loved one needs me urgently?' 'What if I become unwell during the school day?' 'What if there's a fight? A fire? A conflict between colleagues?' I've noticed that in schools where such eventualities are planned for, and policies and procedures are easily accessible, transparent and properly thought-through, overall levels of engagement and wellbeing tend to be higher. Expectations and entitlements need to be absolutely clear – and fairness is key. I noted with a mix of amusement and respect a school with a 'romantic relationships at work' policy, which includes a need to let somebody (but not everybody!) know, an avoidance of any line-management responsibility between those 'involved' and even a section on professional expectations if you split up.

Human beings are simultaneously more predictable than they realise and completely unpredictable. Life happens; people are as vulnerable and flawed as they are brimming with potential to make a lasting difference. Let's turn to the moments that have made a difference to you.

BIOSOCIAL MODEL

As we reflect on life events as they link to professional wellbeing and effectiveness, Engel's biosocial model (1977) is a useful lens through which to consider how we survive and thrive as humans and professionals and what factors might be at play when we struggle.

Picture three legs of a stool – it's important that all three legs of the stool are sturdy and strong for us to be our happiest and most effective. Each leg represents the following key elements:

1 **Biological factors:** Genetics, brain chemistry, and physical health.
2 **Psychological factors**: Emotions, thoughts, behaviours, and mental health.
3 **Social factors:** Relationships, cultural influences, and socio-economic status.

Bearing in mind the importance of focusing on what we can control, here are some ways in which this framework applies to the lives of teachers:

1 Biological factors in teaching:
   o Physical demands of constant movement, standing, and voice projection affect teacher stamina and health.
   o Sleep patterns disrupted by workload and stress directly impact classroom performance and decision-making.
   o Hormone fluctuations from stress response affect energy levels throughout the academic year.
   o Physical health conditions may be exacerbated by workplace demands (e.g. back problems from marking, vocal strain).
   o Brain chemistry affected by constant high-alert status in classroom management.

2 Psychological factors in teaching:
   o Cognitive load from constant decision-making and multitasking in the classroom.
   o Emotional labour of managing both student and parent relationships.
   o Self-efficacy beliefs about teaching ability impact resilience and performance.
   o Anxiety around observations and accountability measures.
   o Mental stamina required for maintaining professional persona.
   o Impact of perceived success/failure on professional identity.

3 Social factors in teaching:
   o Department/faculty relationships affect daily working experience.
   o School leadership and line-management approaches influence job satisfaction and stress levels.

o Parent interactions can be both supportive and challenging.
o Wider education policy changes impact working conditions.
o Status of teaching profession in society affects morale.
o Work–life balance challenges with marking and planning.
o Professional competition and comparison with colleagues.

FOR LEADERS: TARGETING AREAS

The model suggests interventions should target all three areas simultaneously for maximum effectiveness. For example:

- Biological: Ensuring adequate breaks, providing proper equipment for posture, managing timetabling to allow recovery periods.
- Psychological: Offering supervision and coaching, developing resilience strategies, providing clear success criteria.
- Social: Building supportive department cultures, managing workload collectively, creating meaningful collaboration opportunities.

Reflection: Your Biosocial Stool

Use image 8.1 to draw or imagine your own biosocial 'stool'. Which elements of each 'leg' are established and strong? Which are a bit scuffed but still performing their function? What steps can you take to strengthen each leg?

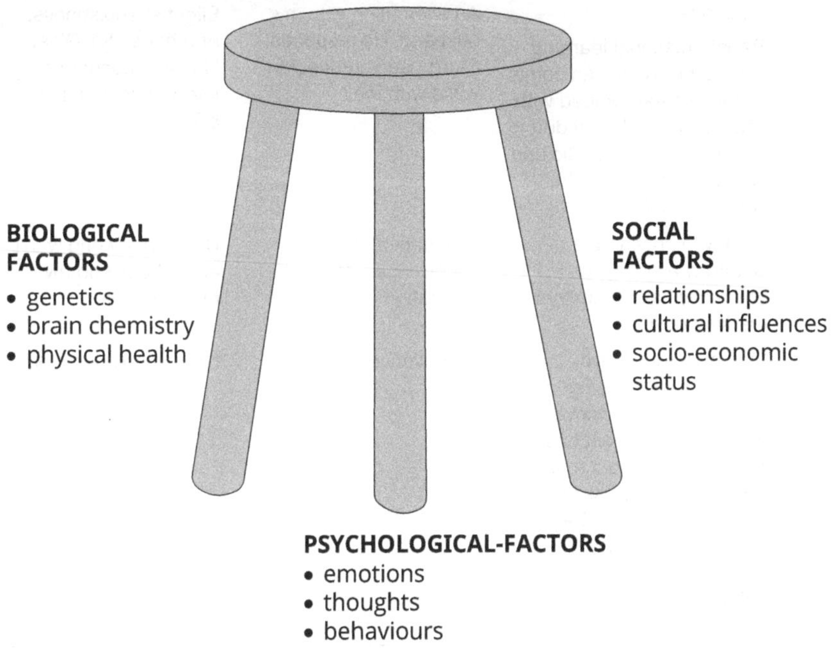

BIOLOGICAL FACTORS
- genetics
- brain chemistry
- physical health

SOCIAL FACTORS
- relationships
- cultural influences
- socio-economic status

PSYCHOLOGICAL-FACTORS
- emotions
- thoughts
- behaviours

Figure 8.1 Biosocial model

CRITICAL INCIDENTS

Critical incidents are significant, challenging or unexpected events that prompt reflection, emotional response, and potential transformation in our professional and personal self-understanding and practice. These incidents, which may seem insignificant at the time, serve as powerful catalysts for professional growth and identity development. They can be transformative, often leading us to confront and re-evaluate our professional identity, pedagogical approaches, and underlying values about education. They carry strong emotional weight, either positive, negative or a mixture of the two, and are an anchor point for memory and reflection.

Here are a few of mine, with reflections – see Table 8.1:

Table 8.1 Emma's Critical Incidents

Year	Incident	Emotions	Transformational learning
1999	I'm a new teacher in conversation with my deputy headteacher. 'I'm surprised at how lonely this job can be. There's nobody to share it with.' His response: 'Share it with the students.'	Reassured, I'm not alone	Transformational learning: feedback comes from lots of important places but the students can provide the most honest, powerful (and usually kind) feedback of all.
2004	Emotions: Transformational learning: my teacher voice can come in handy. Best avoided with immediate family, but during disagreements in traffic and on the streets, it can be carefully deployed.	An altercation with my husband. He responds, 'Don't use your teacher voice with me!'	Slight sheepishness. And honestly? Glee. I have a teacher voice, finally! And it has an effect...
2005	Sofa with husband, a Saturday evening. 'Do you really have to do that marking now?'	Indignation, self-importance – then realisation	Umm. The world won't end if I don't do my marking now.
2008	First maternity leave. I return for a 'Keeping in Touch' day and discover that the department hasn't fallen apart without me. When someone asks for my thoughts on a Key Stage 5 scheme of learning, I realise I have no strong feelings or opinions and am happy for them to decide...	Mild offence, relief	I'm not indispensable!

Year	Incident	Emotions	Transformational learning
2010	Second maternity leave. The ash cloud of Eyjafjallajökull has left many of my colleagues stranded all over the globe, with flights grounded. I go to school to help out and teach with my baby strapped to my front. The students coo and are refreshingly helpful and colleagues help change her nappy at breaktime.	Pride, joy (and I've conveniently blanked out the stress and inconvenience of balancing a baby with 90 teenagers)	Letting my students see me as a whole human being at times (when appropriate) is powerful and important for me.
2015	Youngest daughter, aged 6: 'Mummy, you're the only parent who never comes to our assemblies'.	Pure and all-too-familiar guilt. I'm clearly letting everyone down, all of the time	Ask for the things that are important to you! I have few regrets, but not being brave or assertive enough to ask to attend such events is one. Also, it was empiricaly untrue that I was the only parent not to attend, and I was doing my best…
2017	2017, a conversation with an external consultant about my team's performance: 'You go and tell them it's just not good enough.'	Righteous rage and indignation! I'm so not doing that.	Go with your values and know when they are challenged repeatedly that it might be time to change your context.
2023	I check my phone in between lessons. The ambulance is just arriving. A close relative on her way to hospital. My teacher assistant says, 'Just go. I'll sort the rest.'	Anxiety, distress, a sense of what's important, reassurance that people are looking out for me here.	When you need to go, you need to go!

Reflection: You and Your Critical Incidents

Use Table 8.2 for you to reflect on your critical incident.

Spend some time reflecting on between six and ten key critical incidents in the course of your career in education. At this stage, don't spend too much time worrying about whether they are positive or negative and what that suggests, just jot them down in the first column *Incidents* (in no particular order).

Now use the second column, *Emotions*, to consider what emotions they invoked in you. Surprise, delight, guilt, shock? You may wish to refer to Brackett's table of emotions referenced in Chapter 6.

(Continued)

Now, in the third column, *Transformational Learning*, in a sentence, what was your key learning about yourself, personally and professionally, from each one? How have you applied this learning since?

Table 8.2 You and Your Critical Incidents

Year	Incident	Emotions	Transformational learning

CATACLYSMIC EVENTS

This section comes with a trigger warning – there are references to suicide and tragedies. At the end of this chapter, I have signposted tried and tested contacts who can support you if you're struggling.

If you've been teaching for more than a few years, the chances are you'll have experienced profoundly transformative events too, from significant changes in location and context to life's expected, yet always challenging, transitions – starting a family, falling in love, relationship breakdown, illness, injury and bereavement. Through my career, I've known colleagues and pupils struck down by devastating illness, crises in mental health, and had their realities and expectations overturned by miscarriage, betrayal, debt and natural disaster. I've been part of school communities shattered by suicide, murder and premature death in a range of devastating forms and tried to find the words when meeting their loved one's eyes at their funerals. Whilst few of us will live through a decade completely shielded from such events, individuals' responses vary dramatically.

I've known three parent-educators whose own children have died in the last three years, one to murder, one to a drug overdose and one by suicide. One decided to leave the profession to grieve quietly and privately, before returning a couple of years later having taken a step away from leadership; one cut back her hours and continues in her familiar role quietly and competently; whilst the other has pursued a path to headship – there is clearly no right and wrong path and there are no pithy lessons to be derived from such tragedy. I spoke to one of these parents in preparation for this book – she wishes the details of her situation to be kept vague and anonymous. 'What lessons can colleagues learn?' I asked her.

- Talk to me about my child, she said – don't pretend she never existed.
- Don't make assumptions about how I 'should' be feeling. One colleague told me I was no fun anymore and questioned why I no longer attend parties.
- Signposting support can be helpful – but don't push it. I found a support group that works for me and it's been, quite literally, a lifesaver.
- There's so much I used to dwell on and worry about that, since my daughter's death, really doesn't matter. I have a much clearer idea of what really matters.

Case Study: Zara

From TA to Teacher – A Journey Through Adversity

While working as a TA, I received a breast cancer diagnosis through an early mammogram programme. At the time, my son was preparing for important exams and I was also caring for my daughters at home. Two operations confirmed it was Grade 3 and I began chemotherapy. I left school at the end of the summer term, uncertain when I would return, but determined not to dwell on the 'what if.'

During treatment, especially radiotherapy, I began planning a phased return, and was back full time by the end of April. The experience was both physically and mentally transformative. I loved my work and I realised I wanted more, and that I was capable of more. I decided to pursue teaching.

Soon afterwards, a new teacher started to treat me more like a PA than a TA, clearly threatened. I already had a degree but had put my career on hold due to family commitments and a controlling relationship. With encouragement and a renewed sense of purpose, I applied for a teacher training programme.

My initial application was unsuccessful. The head told me, 'I suggest you look for a career outside of working with children.' It was a crushing moment, but I didn't give up. I was accepted onto a SCITT programme at another school within the trust.

During my SCITT placement, a teaching role became available. I applied and was successful. I recently left that post after challenges with leadership, but I carry with me years of life experience that shape my approach in the classroom. My teaching career may be relatively new, but it's built on decades of personal resilience.

Cancer took my mum – my biggest supporter – but I refused to let it take anything else. I chose to change the narrative and turn my experience into something empowering.

Case Study: Francesca

My Dad Died. I Was Told I'd 'Let My Students Down'

I started my teaching career at a supportive school, moving across the country for the role. The headteacher was compassionate and made it clear that family came first. When my dad became seriously ill, I was allowed time to visit and help care for him. Despite this, my attendance remained excellent, and I was deeply committed to my students.

When the head left, her deputy took over and quickly became distant, introducing sudden restructures and increasing pressure. Not long after, I got the call that my dad was deteriorating and might not survive. I followed procedure and asked for time off – but was told, 'You can have three days off for the funeral.' Despite my pleading, she refused to budge.

A colleague advised me to get a sick note, which I did. I travelled home in distress, continued marking work, and cared for my dad until he passed away. Even then, I received cold emails questioning my return. When I went back, I expected support – instead, I was told I'd 'let my students down.' The cover teacher was praised and I was told to buy them a gift. My commitment was questioned, and I felt judged and undermined.

My mental health suffered. I was injured intervening in a serious incident and later told I'd been left to manage alone as a form of punishment. Still, I didn't want to leave, but I handed in my notice early to be considerate. The head then refused to write me a reference, something she'd done to others too. Thankfully, my former head and colleagues supported me.

I took a step down in role and pay just to get out and recover. It's taken almost a decade, but I'm now a head of year and doing well. I still carry some anxiety, but I've rebuilt my career. That experience changed me – but it didn't break me.

Case Study: Sonya

My Students Saved Me

At 23 weeks, my baby son died.

There's no easy way to say it – and no way to separate that loss from my identity as a teacher.

I started teaching at 23, full of purpose, convinced I could change lives. More than a decade later, I found myself co-teaching A-Level English with a newly qualified colleague, building a course from scratch after the disruption of the pandemic.

My group – six brilliant, curious students – became my anchor. We read Keats, Atwood, and Williams. I watched them grow in confidence, finding their voices in literature. What they didn't know was that they were also helping me rebuild. In the middle of grief, the classroom gave me something to hold onto.

When I left for maternity leave again, this time with hope and a healthy baby on the way, I felt a pang saying goodbye. That summer, they returned, clutching their results – and all six found their next steps. We thanked each other.

I used to think I went into teaching to save others.

Now I know: in my darkest days, it was my students who saved me.

TEACHING DURING TIMES OF CRISIS

Another hugely humbling experience recently came when I was researching the wellbeing of teachers during the war in Ukraine for a paper, 'Teacher wellbeing and self-care during times of crisis', that I wrote for the OECD (2024). The three educators I interviewed (one young teacher and two more experienced leaders) were utterly pragmatic, motivated by a profound sense of moral purpose and a clear focus on the controllables. When I probed into the personal impact on her, Nataliia, a school leader, shifted the focus: 'If I start crying – if everybody starts crying – how does it help? No, it won't help. We say, this is our job. Teachers teach and doctors treat people' (Kell, 2024b, p.14).

Whilst acknowledging that teaching during wartime is inevitably stressful and exhausting, Maria, who'd moved from the private sector to the state sector at the start of the war, said:

> *The fact is that we do have to influence education because that is our future. We are undergoing an active state of war and that's hard, but after that will come the rebuilding of Ukraine. [...] Those kids who are currently at schools, they're going to join us as adults in society and it's our responsibility to shape the adults that we would like to [rebuild] our society.* (Kell, 2024b, p.9)

Whilst reflecting on the deaths of former students in conflict (five when I first contacted her, six when the paper went to publication), Nataliia focused on what can be done: 'What can we do? We can only make sure we go to the funerals and offer support to the parents' (Kell, 2024b, p.13).

Whilst oversimplification is unhelpful – I am in no way qualified to consider the level of trauma these people are going through – I found conducting this research deeply humbling and illuminating. Those of us here in the UK can take valuable lessons, I believe, from the pragmatism, collaboration and resounding values of those educating during times of conflict. The key to their sense of wellbeing, as they process immediate and ongoing crisis, is a shared sense of moral purpose.

OUR ROLE IN OUR STUDENTS' LIVES

Teaching is far more than curriculum delivery – it's a human profession rooted in connection, compassion, and care. Teachers are often the steady presence in a young person's life, quietly building their confidence, affirming their worth, and helping them navigate the stormier seasons of childhood and adolescence. From celebrating their smallest wins to standing beside them in moments of unimaginable grief, we play a vital role in shaping not just their academic outcomes but their sense of identity and resilience. As Jaz Ampaw-Farr movingly shares in her TEDx talk, *The power of everyday heroes'* it was the ordinary, consistent kindness of her teachers that changed the course of her life. Every encouraging word, every act of empathy – these are the moments that linger and shape the adults our students become. This is one of the many things that make our job such a unique privilege.

Case Study: More than a Lesson

Being there When it Matters Most

It was a normal school day, until I got a message from the pastoral team urgently asking me to collect a Year 10 student and her sister in sixth form. Their mother was on her way in to tell them that their father had died suddenly in a road accident that morning.

I waited outside the science hall, heart in my throat, trying to stay calm. I told the student we needed to go to the head's office. When she asked why, I simply said she'd find out when we got there.

Inside, her mother, sister, the head, and head of sixth form were waiting. I stayed outside with the others. Minutes later, we heard the girls screaming – it was devastating. Everyone in the outer office, from senior staff to admin, was visibly shaken. We all just wanted to protect them, to somehow make it better.

Later that day, we brought together their closest friends to share the news and offer support. The school made it clear that their mother wasn't alone – we would be there for all of them.

I went home and hugged my own children tightly. That day has never left me. It reminded me that schools are so much more than places of learning. We are part of the fabric of our students' lives. We support, care, and show up when it matters most.

Case Study: Ella

A Lesson in Perspective

I've been teaching pupils with severe and complex learning difficulties for over a decade, with much of that time spent supporting those with profound additional needs. At first, it was daunting, but over time, it became where I truly felt at home.

Teaching children with complex medical conditions, physical disabilities, and sensory impairments pushed me to adapt and think creatively every single day.

One pupil in particular had a rare life-limiting condition. Let's call her Ella. Despite the prognosis often associated with her diagnosis, she started school at four years old, full of curiosity and joy. Tiny in stature, with a huge personality and a smile that could light up the room, Ella reminded us daily of the beauty in small moments. Her family were warm, appreciative, and embraced each day they had with her.

As it happened, I was pregnant while teaching Ella, and I remember being struck by how clinical and bleak the medical literature could be when discussing conditions like hers. But there Ella was, thriving, learning, and living her school life to the fullest.

Sadly, her health declined. When I said goodbye to her at the end of the school year, I had a gut feeling it might be the last time. Midway through the summer, I was told she'd been placed on end-of-life care. With the family's invitation, my teaching assistant and I visited her at home. We sat peacefully with her parents for hours, sharing stories, laughter, and quiet moments. It wasn't a sad visit – it was a privilege.

Her parents told us how proud they were that Ella got to have her first day of school, that she wore her uniform, and that she was part of something. They talked about how much she loved swimming and how tired she'd be after a school day. They were grateful she had the chance to learn and be included.

That visit changed me. Whenever I question the value of our work, or hear others doubt the purpose of teaching pupils with significant needs, I think of Ella. Every child deserves access to education, no matter how short or complex their life may be. I'm honoured to be part of theirs.

IMPACT OF LIFE-CHANGING EVENTS

Whether it's moving house, a change of relationship, the loss of a loved one, or a significant interaction, life events can have a huge impact on the motivation and performance of educators – both negatively and positively and usually a mixture of the two.

Negative Effects

- Emotional stress from significant life changes can temporarily reduce teaching effectiveness and classroom presence. During periods of intense grief or major transition, educators may struggle to maintain their usual energy levels and emotional availability for students and colleagues, potentially affecting the learning environment.
- Physical and mental exhaustion, particularly during early parenthood, whilst processing grief, or managing a move, can impact lesson planning and classroom organisation. Sleep deprivation and divided attention may lead to

decreased productivity and creativity in developing educational materials and activities.

- Career disruption and scheduling challenges often arise during major life transitions. Educators may need to take extended leaves of absence, adjust their working hours, or even change positions, which can interrupt key relationships and curriculum continuity.
- Financial stress associated with life changes like moving or starting a family can force educators to take on additional work, potentially reducing the time and energy they can invest in their primary teaching responsibilities. This added pressure may affect their ability to participate in extra-curricular activities or professional development opportunities.

Positive Effects

- Personal growth through life experiences often translates directly into enhanced empathy and understanding in the classroom. For example, an educator who has experienced bereavement may develop deeper compassion for students going through similar situations and create more supportive learning environments during difficult times.
- Major life transitions like parenthood can bring new perspectives on child development and learning styles. For example, parents often report gaining invaluable insights into how children think, learn, and process emotions, which they can apply to their teaching methodology and classroom management.
- Relocating to a new area can expand an educator's cultural awareness and bring fresh teaching approaches. Moving house often exposes teachers to different communities and educational systems, leading to innovative classroom strategies and broader cultural perspectives they can share with students.

FOR LEADERS: MANAGING A SCHOOL'S CAPACITY TO SUPPORT STAFF THROUGH CHALLENGING TIMES

Whilst it is well worth having policies which plan for how the school will support and signpost support for those going through challenging or transformative times, it's also worth noting that everyone's reaction will be unique to them. Whilst one person may need (reasonable) time away from work to support others or themselves, another may well take comfort in the psychological security, sense of moral purpose and routines of working in a school.

It's also important to acknowledge that, whilst our instinct might be to prioritise compassion and give staff indefinite time away when they're struggling, one of the biggest strains on schools' capacity (including the financial hit) is staff absence – unlike in many other workplaces, none of us is easily replicable on a day-to-day basis and the need to 'cover' for absent colleagues can be hugely stressful, often resulting in other staff going off as the result of the stress incurred – a vicious cycle.

Here are some tips which have worked effectively in other schools:

- **Apply structured flexibility:** Allow temporary role changes (e.g. swapping duties) while upholding essential safety and learning standards.
- **Establish reliable cover systems:** Keep a pool of trusted supply staff, set up internal cover arrangements, and use clear handover notes to ensure continuity during absences.
- **Support phased returns:** Ease staff back in with a gradual build-up of responsibilities, starting with lighter tasks to support a smooth transition.
- **Set clear boundaries during challenging periods:** Temporarily reduce non-essential duties and define timeframes to help manage workload effectively.
- **Promote a supportive culture:** Train middle leaders in sensitive conversations, encourage peer support, and maintain open communication about the impact of support measures.
- **Refine practices through experience:** Review what works, adapt policies, and create role-specific contingency plans based on lessons learned.

KEY FACTORS AFFECTING EDUCATORS' MOTIVATION

Taking time to consider the factors which affect educators' motivation is essential, particularly as we face a worldwide shortage of teachers. The following factors are worth considering:

- **Confidence:** Feeling capable and assured in teaching, decision-making, and managing the classroom boosts motivation and retention.
- **Commitment:** A strong dedication to teaching and ongoing development encourages long-term engagement in the profession.
- **Resilience:** The ability to adapt and recover from setbacks supports sustained motivation and personal wellbeing.
- **Happiness:** Positive feelings about work, achievements, and relationships at school enhance job satisfaction and the desire to remain in post.
- **Self-efficacy:** Belief in one's ability to influence pupil learning strengthens purpose and persistence in the role.
- **Work–life balance:** Managing the demands of work alongside personal life helps prevent burnout and supports a sustainable career in teaching.

Reflection: Factors Affecting Your Motivation

If you were to score yourself on a scale of 1–10 (with 10 being the highest and best) in each of the areas above, what score would you give? What tweaks might you make to increase your score in key areas?

If you were to place these factors in order of how important they are to you, what might this look like for you at the moment? How might the order have changed over the years?

EDUCATION: A JOB OR A LIFESTYLE?

Another memory – an experienced and respected colleague gives his retirement speech to all staff. In it, he tells us, 'remember, this is just a job. A wonderful job, but just a job,' before he sets off to spend time travelling, with his grandchildren, on his garden (one of the many people I know who find a busier life in retirement than when they're employed). Whist I'm not sure I necessarily agree with the term 'just a job' (any more than I agree with someone who describes themselves as 'just' a teacher, teaching assistant, etc.), it was another pivotal moment for me during a time when I was utterly absorbed in and subsumed by my work and so closely associated everything about it with my value as a human being.

What is clear from working with colleagues feeling under-the-weather, in the later stages of pregnancy or just not 'firing on all cylinders' on a particular day is how hard it is to take a foot off the pedal. Whilst children can show remarkable empathy, en masse, their needs and demands don't reduce in proportion to our capacity, so our jobs can frequently demand depths of energy and attention that leave us at the end of the day barely able to string a sentence together – so 'balance' can be a tricky one to achieve!

For me and so many of the educators I've had the honour of getting to know, being a teacher, a teaching assistant, or a school leader forms a core part of their identity. It's a source of pride, self-worth, earned status in the community. A reminder at this point that nothing in this book (or in any of my work) is about telling you what you should and shouldn't do – as my now-teens would say, 'you do you'. It is, however, well worth considering to what extent your job as an educator is part of who you are – and how this might change or have changed in the course of your career.

I find when I look at it from this perspective that my job tends to take over more of my life than I'd like to imagine. If I find myself with an unexpected few 'spare' hours, rather than losing myself in a leisure activity, I'll catch myself heading towards my desk. My kids recently banned me from talking to their friends about school – 'Mum, stop being such a teacher!'. Whilst I feel blessed to have a job that fills me with passion and enthusiasm, it's a pertinent reminder that establishing – and constantly re-establishing – healthy boundaries is key.

Reflection: To What Extent Does Your Career as an Educator Constitute Your Identity?

Have a look at the dial in Figure 8.2, which includes a scale from 1–10. Remember, there's no 'right' or 'wrong' answer – only what works for you and your life at present. With 1–2 representing 'just a job' and 9–10 representing a lifestyle, where would you place yourself at the moment?

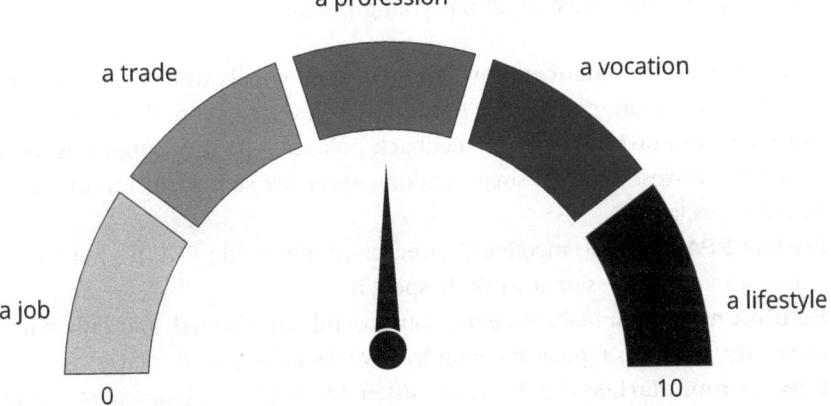

Figure 8.2 Teaching and your identity

Now consider where you'd *like* to be. What minor tweaks or changes might help you get there?

ESTABLISHING HEALTHY BOUNDARIES

Let's never forget we're public servants – professionals who owe it to ourselves and our communities to do the best job we can for our young people. But we can't do it if we're 'worn-out husks' (Kell, 2024a) and, frankly, our young people value mentally healthy and rounded human beings.

- **Set clear work hours:** Your classroom isn't open 24/7. Set and stick to office hours – then switch off at the end of the day. The to-do list can wait.
- **Protect your breaks:** Eat lunch away from your desk. Step out, chat with colleagues, or enjoy a quiet moment – your wellbeing depends on it.
- **Know your role:** Be compassionate, not a counsellor. Support pupils, but signpost to appropriate services when needed.
- **Simplify marking:** Use efficient approaches like whole-class feedback and peer assessment. Feedback matters – but it doesn't need to be an essay.

- **Keep one day sacred:** Take at least one full day off each week. No emails, no planning – just rest and recharge. You'll be better for it.

MODELLING HEALTHY BOUNDARIES AS A SCHOOL LEADER

If you are a school leader, paying careful attention to school culture and supporting your staff to maintain healthy boundaries is key. After all, a teaching team running on empty helps no one, least of all our young people.

- **Model work–life balance:** Leave on time, keep emails within working hours, and share non-work plans. Your example sets the tone more than any policy.
- **Cut back on marking:** Review feedback policies – do they support learning or just tick boxes? Promote smart marking and back staff against unrealistic parent expectations.
- **Protect PPA time:** No meetings, cover, or admin during PPA. It's not 'free' time – it's vital professional work. Respect it.
- **Rethink meetings:** Make meetings purposeful, time-bound, and only when necessary. Consider regular meeting-free weeks to help staff focus.
- **Respect boundaries:** If staff say no, listen and trust their judgement. Avoid quick fixes – sometimes they just need to feel heard and supported.

LIFE PHASES OF EDUCATORS

It's well worth turning to the work of Christopher Day et al. (2006), who in their study argued that quality retention of teachers is enhanced by an understanding of their strengths and needs during different 'phases' of their careers.

It's worth noting, 20 years on, that the study, which took place between 2001 and 2005, was conducted at a time when there was still the widely held belief that most of us would have just one main 'career' in the course of our lives.

Recent research from the World Economic Forum (Broom, 2023) suggests that lifetime employment in a single job is a thing of the past, due to factors including the rising cost of living, the need to work for longer and the impact of the pandemic, which led an increasing number of people to seek a higher degree of flexibility, greater pay or even, simply, more enjoyment in their work. With changing attitudes through different generations, our younger generations seem less willing to 'suck it up' and tolerate working environments which don't match their values and priorities (Francis, 2022).

So, with likely variations in mind, let's consider Day et al.'s six 'life phases' of teaching, which I've captured in my own words below.

Years 1–3: The Early Years

A period of steep learning and emotional fluctuation. Planning is time consuming, self doubt is frequent, but positive feedback from pupils offers moments of reassurance and motivation.

Years 4–7: Building Confidence

Teaching skills become more refined, and classroom management strengthens. Confidence grows, and teachers begin to take on additional responsibilities while developing a clearer professional identity.

Years 8–15: Reflection and Reassessment

Efficiency increases with experience, but questions about long-term direction may arise. Some pursue leadership, others reaffirm their place in the classroom. Work–life balance becomes a greater priority.

Years 16–23: Consolidation and Challenge

Professional confidence is well-established. While experience allows for smoother day-to-day teaching, ongoing reforms and shifting expectations can feel draining. Mentoring newer colleagues becomes a rewarding focus.

Years 24–30: Seasoned Professionalism

Judgement is trusted, instincts are sharp, and contributions are valued. While adapting to change may feel more demanding, many teachers find renewed energy in shaping school culture and guiding others.

30+ Years: Legacy and Transition

With a wealth of experience and a lasting impact on pupils and colleagues alike, these teachers are key figures in school life. Focus shifts to passing on knowledge, supporting the next generation, and leaving a meaningful legacy.

Reflection: Life Phases

As you read the six phases, which do you most closely relate to? One or a combination of different ones?

What proportion of your colleagues might fit into each 'phase'? What does this suggest about your community?

Do people have others in similar phases they can relate to in work or are there some 'outliers'? What are the implications of this?

Day's research identifies one of the most critical periods as being teachers of 8–15 years' experience. This core group, which has the potential to bring wisdom, energy and experience to schools, is one for whom quality professional development is key to maintaining motivation. This group also frequently has significant commitments outside the school building. Retaining those in this group who wish to remain in the profession is key.

PARENTS WHO TEACH

The MTPT (Maternity Teacher/Paternity Teacher) project, led by the indomitable Emma Sheppard, has, since 2016, been highlighting the impact of motherhood, more recently including perspectives from fatherhood, on teacher retention. Its 'Missing mothers' report (McShane and Sheppard, 2024) highlights the fact that mothers in their 30s represent the single biggest group leaving teaching, with student behaviour and workload creating a 'vicious cycle' whereby the departure of committed and experienced teachers exacerbates the problem. It identifies flexibility (around timetabling and working hours) as key to retaining mother-teachers. Based on the work of the MTPT project and my own doctoral research (Kell, 2016), here are some tips on surviving and thriving as a parent and educator.

Set Clear Boundaries

Keep schoolwork in its place – ideally in a dedicated space you can walk away from. Your teaching bag stays zipped until you're ready (report season excluded!). Use your planning skills at home too –try a family whiteboard to map out the week.

Build a Parent–Teacher Network

Connect with colleagues who understand the juggle – like the one sprinting to nursery at 5:30. Share childcare, swap tips, and never apologise for leaving on time. Efficiency isn't laziness – it's survival.

Use Your Dual Role

Your teaching skills work at home, and parenting makes you a more empathetic teacher. You *get* behaviour struggles and sleepless nights – use that insight to connect with pupils and parents alike.

Prioritise Your Wellbeing

Book your own parents' evening slots early, use PPA time wisely, and carve out guilt-free downtime. Whether it's a solo coffee or ten quiet minutes with a book – make it non-negotiable.

FOR LEADERS: GETTING THE BEST OUT OF TEACHER-PARENT COLLEAGUES

Set Boundaries with Flexibility

Define non-negotiables like safeguarding and teaching hours, but allow flexibility elsewhere – e.g. adaptable PPA use or split parents' evenings, provided standards remain high.

Prioritise Predictability

Advance notice of dates and deadlines helps teacher-parents manage childcare and workload. When changes are unavoidable, communicate clearly and offer support.

Value their Skill Set

Parenting sharpens time management, problem-solving, and empathy. Involve teacher-parents in mentoring, pastoral care, and parent communication – these are strengths, not limitations.

Focus on Outcomes, Not Hours

Encourage efficiency over presenteeism. Trust teacher-parents to manage their time well and develop sustainable work patterns. Their strategies often benefit the whole team.

Foster Open Communication

Regular check-ins help address issues early. Offer targeted support during peak times, and trust teacher-parents to balance their roles professionally – they often hold themselves to the highest standards.

Reflection: Three Key Questions

Having been through a fairly challenging 'life happens' kind of couple of years, I found myself trying to extricate myself from what felt increasingly messy in terms of competing priorities and the range of emotions to which they gave rise. I focused, for my TEDx talk of 2024, on three big but simple questions, which I'll end this chapter by asking you. If you step back and look at where you are now, at your work and what's currently important in your life, how would you answer the following?

1 What do you need (practically, emotionally, psychologically, environmentally) to feel truly happy and successful?
2 What do you want your legacy to be?
3 What does 'good enough' look like for you in the different spheres of your life and work?

CONCLUSION

As we navigate the inevitable twists and turns of life, it's crucial to remember that our professional roles are deeply intertwined with our personal experiences. By acknowledging and planning for these significant events, we can support ourselves and each other more effectively. Let's embrace the messiness of working with human beings, knowing that our resilience and compassion are what truly make a lasting difference. Reflect on your journey, support your colleagues, and continue to grow both personally and professionally. Life happens, and together, with wisdom, self-awareness and compassion, we can, not just survive, but thrive.

REFERENCES

Ampaw-Farr, J. (2017). 'The power of everyday heroes'. *TEDx Talk*, 30 March. TEDx Norwich.

Broom, D. (2023). 'Having many careers will be the norm, experts say'. *World Economic Forum*, 2 May. www.weforum.org/stories/2023/05/workers-multiple-careers-jobs-skills/#:~:text=%E2%80%9CLifetime%20employment%20at%20a%20single,those%20attitudes%20are%20quickly%20changing.%E2%80%9D

Day, C., Sammons, P., Stobart, G., Kington, A. and Gu, Q. (2006). *Variations in Teachers' Work, Lives and their Effects on Pupils (VITAE): The key findings*. British Educational Research Association (BERA) Annual Conference.

Engel, G. L. (1977). The need for a new medical model: A challenge for biomedicine. *Science*, 196(4286), 129–136.

Francis, A. (2022). 'Gen Z: The workers who want it all'. *BBC Worklife*, 14 June. www.bbc.com/worklife/article/20220613-gen-z-the-workers-who-want-it-all

Kell, E. (2016). *Shifting identities: A mixed methods study of the experiences of teachers who are also parents* (Thesis). Middlesex University. https://repository.mdx.ac.uk/download/1036d0ec083ce6353007738348b9b7946402df67fe8d9b5671fb5f1cbc08c831/3958117/EKellThesis.pdf

Kell, E. (2024a). 'Taking control and reducing the risk of burnout' [TEDx talk]. *TEDx Kingston*, 14 January. www.youtube.com/watch?v=q4ZEoYM3zHw

Kell, E. (2024b). 'Teacher wellbeing and self-care during times of crisis: Foundational insights for the OECD teaching compass'. OECD. www.oecd.org/content/dam/oecd/en/about/projects/edu/education-2040/global-forum/6th-global-forum/Emma_Kell_Teacher_Wellbeing_and_Self-Care_During_Times_of_Crisis.pdf

McShane, A. and Sheppard, E. (2024). *Missing mothers*. The New Britain Project & MTPT Project. www.newbritain.org.uk/_files/ugd/8be189_06c43a81df034e6598475e2b888b0c96.pdf

Contacts for If You're Struggling – Or Would Simply Benefit from Some External Support

Education Support: www.educationsupport.org.uk
SANDS: Saving Babies' Lives. Supporting Bereaved Families: www.sands.org.uk
SOBS: Survivors of Bereavement by Suicide: https://uksobs.com
Talking Heads Supervision: https://talkingheadssupervision.co.uk
The Samaritans: www.samaritans.org/how-we-can-help/contact-samaritan

9

SAYING GOODBYE

This chapter explores:

- **Reflections on goodbyes:** Personal experiences and memories of farewells in a teaching career.
- **Impactful departures:** The significance of leaving a school and the emotional impact on both the departing and those left behind.
- Practical advice for leaders on **organising farewells**.
- **Exit interviews:** Their importance and suggested questions for exit interviews.
- **Why goodbyes matter:** The emotional and practical significance of farewells.

MY STORY: REFLECTIONS ON MY GOODBYES

As I sit to write this chapter, my mind is filled with the goodbyes I've experienced and witnessed in my 26 years as a teacher, from the hollow and lonely sudden or surreptitious departures though the car park to the truly fulfilling and rewarding final pages of colourful and exciting chapters. I'm picturing a chaotic picnic with children and families on Hampstead Heath, marking the end of an era with a CD I'd made for every student, including Green Day's 'Good Riddance' and Louis Armstrong's 'We Have All the Time in the World'. Referencing these songs for this work has them playing in the background, and they evoke such a bittersweet mix of pride and sadness at the inevitable passing of time. I have the unique privilege of still being in touch with many of these former students, now in their mid-thirties. These memories stand as a regular reminder of what a huge joy and privilege this job is.

Reflection: Music as a Reminder

Think of a chapter that closed for you recently in your career in teaching. Is there a song or piece which captures the mood of that chapter for you? What emotions does it evoke?

It strikes me that it is almost ten years to the day that I left the school which, arguably, had the most significant impact on my development and identity as an educator. The series of events which led up to my departure were pretty tumultuous (in hindsight, involving lots of quite unnecessary drama). I'd been for an internal role (the equivalent to the role I'd already been doing), messed up the interview, sobbed on a filthy carpet in my friend and colleague's office, declared myself 'done' and thrown myself into seeking fresh pastures (no, the grass wasn't greener, but that's another story and all part of the growing process). But actually, the eight years I'd spent there had been predominantly joyful and rewarding ones. The school had flourished, growing from one where the corridors reeked of urine and suspiciously fragrant smoke to one which exuded colour and purpose, and I had grown with it, as a teacher, as a leader and as a human – I'd had both of my children during my time there, and been extremely well-supported. I'd made friendships which endure to this day and will undoubtedly endure for decades more.

I'll be honest, I'm not great with goodbyes. I love a bit of ceremony and celebration but, like many I've come to know in teaching, counterintuitive as it sounds, being centre of attention outside the classroom brings out my instinctive desire to hide in a dark corner. In fact, I've been known, after shorter assignments with less fulfilling endings, to skulk out through the back door after a few quiet farewells, before the festivities commenced.

But here we were. I was one of a handful of staff heading off into the sunset, and the thought that had gone into the event was humbling and moving. Banners, streamers, every member of staff in the large, airy canteen on a sunny-but-fresh kind of a day. Few things happen in schools without something unexpected occurring, and lo and behold, there was an exam happening on the floor below, so we had to be super-quiet.

My farewell speech was delivered by a colleague I treasured and contained the perfect mix of gentle fun and genuine respect and gratitude, referencing my bloopers and my proudest moments with thoughtfulness that touches me as much today as it did in that moment. The exam meant that clapping wasn't an option, so instead, the staff opted for a BSL goodbye: they all waved in my direction at the same time in a beautiful moment that will stay with me forever.

I remember another goodbye with the same sort of warmth and gratitude. Our headteacher, a reserved man not prone to grand gestures or sentimentality, had, for each of us leaving, clearly gone carefully through our time at the school and picked out key moments and characteristics to emphasise, leaving us feeling seen, heard and appreciated.

Somewhere in an old computer room in an inner-London borough is a timecapsule, left hidden behind a wooden panel by me and my tutor group, who were moving on at the same time as I did. It contains a ping pong ball, a paper aeroplane and a no-doubt fossilised chocolate bar. It was a silly, childlike act (the best thing about teaching is that we get to channel our inner child) but it was also important and symbolic. It said 'we were here'; it said, 'here is the mark we choose to leave'; it said 'this period was important to us and will stay with us'.

GOODBYES TO TEACHERS: THE BEST AND SOME OF THE WORST

My interactions too, this summer, are dominated by the experiences of those who've recently moved on – leaving the profession for fresh adventures or moving between schools. The hiatus of the summer break offers what for educators is an unusual window for reflection and processing. For those who've left feeling 'special' and 'loved', these are precious times indeed. The stories of songs and poems written and performed for them, speeches, letters, flowers and quiet drop-ins to say 'thank you for the difference you've made and there'll be a you-shaped hole in September' are humbling and moving. They represent memories which will remain until and beyond retirement as reminders that educators' contributions are valued and appreciated. There's a heartwarming video that garnered widespread admiration online in July 2024. It beautifully captures the emotional moment when a beloved teacher in Chesham is honoured with a walk through an arch of staff and students. The scene is filled with applause, smiles, and tears of joy, celebrating an awe-inspiring 47 years of dedication to the school (@CGSBucks). What strikes me about this video is that there is, in fact, apparently minimal 'fuss' involved – it's a relatively simple activity, lasting only a few minutes with no evidence of cost or extravagance but with an emphasis on human connection.

At the other end of the spectrum, I've read and heard some heartbreaking stories of staff left feeling unacknowledged and unappreciated as they exit the school gates for the final time. Sometimes the biggest impact isn't from action – but from inaction. Headteacher Vic Goddard posted on X about his sister and had an overwhelming response, over 7 million views and thousands of responses expressing indignation and frequently direct empathy. The post read as follows (reproduced with permission):

> *My sister retired from teaching today after 38 years in the classroom in one school. No one from SLT spoke to her. No staff gathering organised at all. A card – that's it. She dedicated herself to her craft. Turned down promotions. Wanted to be a great history teacher.* (Goddard, 2024)

My inbox is, I'm afraid, full of similar stories. People left feeling that their efforts over months or years are unappreciated and ignored. Whilst one instinct might be to assume malicious intent, I somehow doubt it's this – I suspect it's more likely to be a case of an omission; a gap when it came to designating and taking on responsibility for co-ordinating leaving events; a case of people simply feeling 'too busy' or overwhelmed and losing sight of the things that, arguably, matter most. We work with human capital, and I'd argue that it's as important to put time, effort and planning into these relationships as it is into a robust assessment framework.

TIP FOR LEADERS: FAREWELLS

Farewells come at the most inconvenient of times. You're exhausted; everyone's exhausted. Your energies are going into making sure everything is in place for the term, semester or year ahead so you can at least justify a few days off for yourself, and you're dealing with the physical and emotional messiness that always comes before school holidays. You know who's leaving but, let's face it, events co-ordinator isn't a job you signed up for and the final day will come – and it will go. It's also true that our former staff are ambassadors – and ideally advocates – for our schools and that the stories they tell will be coloured by how they feel on that final day. Here are some things that can be done to ensure everyone leaves with dignity and a positive conclusion, regardless of what a rollercoaster it might have been up to now.

- Firstly, it doesn't have to be you! You can designate responsibility for all of the below to one key person – or a few key people.
- Many people might want to take charge of any events surrounding their leaving – from organising a meal/drinks to deciding who does their speech; having a sense of control during what is inevitably an emotional time is powerful, so (again, within reason), let them go for it.
- Talk to the person who's leaving to find out what kind of departure they'd like (within reason). Some will want bells and whistles – but more may want a quiet event without fuss or being centre of attention.
- A few words about each person leaving are worth having – could be a speech, a video or something in writing, but whichever you go for, make sure it's composed and delivered by someone who knows the person well and has a positive relationship with them.
- Find out why they're moving on – avoid and challenge speculation and assumption. Facts are your friends.

EXIT INTERVIEWS

It's hugely valuable for the individual and the school for departing staff to have the chance to sit down with a senior member of staff, governor, trustee or well-being lead to formally acknowledge their departure and the factors which have led to it.

Whilst I acknowledge that these can be complex and sometimes thorny, a formal and well-organised process can have a calming effect when emotions are running high. Perhaps most importantly, if they are conducted effectively, they can bust unhelpful assumptions on either side, offer important 'closure' for the staff member and valuable lessons for the school moving forward.

Whilst we know reasons for leaving are many and varied and these would need to be adapted to each unique context, here are some suggestions for what you might want to cover in the exit interviews.

Suggested Exit Interview Questions (to be Adapted to Each Unique Context)

1 How will you remember your time here?
2 What led you to decide to move on?
3 What's your greatest achievement?
4 Who or what has had the biggest positive influence on you?
5 Do you feel you had all the tools you needed to succeed?
6 What suggestions do you have for us?
7 What (if anything) could we have done to keep you?

You may also wish to cover areas like communication, leadership, conditions, workload, work–life balance, but keeping it simple is key.

Exit Interviewers

Choosing carefully who conducts these is also crucial – if you want full honesty, where and how are you likely to receive it? And, perhaps most importantly, what are you going to *do* with the information received, because if the answer is 'nothing' then it becomes a tokenistic and pointless exercise.

When receiving this kind of feedback, it's especially important to depersonalise – the reality is that people often leave because of a strained relationship with an individual or group of individuals. Focusing on behaviours that people find challenging rather than individuals themselves is key.

Face-to-face is always best, I'd argue, but some schools do send out a questionnaire instead and, where departures are reasonably straightforward, some staff welcome these, so this is equally an option – but I'd advocate keeping the door open for an in-person interview where possible.

WHY ARE GOODBYES IMPORTANT?

Goodbyes hold a profound significance for human beings, as they mark the end of a chapter and the beginning of a new one. They are essential for closure, reflection, and the emotional processing of transitions. Goodbyes are not just about the act of leaving; they are about the stories we tell, the memories we create, and the impact we leave behind. They help us make sense of our experiences and provide a sense of closure and continuity in our lives. Whether an educator has spent months or decades in a school, the experience will forever be part of their story – on a purely practical level, the accounts and anecdotes those who leave share about your school will have an impact in the local and wider educational community.

> ### Reflection: Memories of the School where you Teach
>
> When people leave your school, what kinds of things would you like them to be remembering, feeling, thinking and saying?
>
> (This question isn't just for leaders but for all in a school community because ultimately, the stories people tell affect us all.)

PERSPECTIVE AND THE STORIES WE TELL OURSELVES

In my experience, teachers (including myself) can be masters of catastrophising and self-flagellation when things don't go according to plan, so this quote by Oliver Burkeman is one I keep to hand:

> *Most of what troubles us turns out to be tolerable, or even wonderful, or just never happens at all. Next time you worry that something's going to ruin your life, it's worth remembering that if you'd ever been right about that before, even once, your life would presently be ruined.* (Burkeman, 2017)

In coaching, we often talk about framing and reframing the stories we tell ourselves and one another. This isn't about rewriting history or painting over the cracks, but about promoting a healthy sense of perspective and muting the gleeful gremlin on our shoulder which dances and proclaims that this or that incident is just *proof* that you're a rubbish teacher or human being.

It's also about drawing a line or closing a loop because unclosed loops in our minds can turn into tangled clumps in our heads, take up loads of intellectual and emotional energy and cause all manner of havoc. Reframing narratives is also about imposing a healthy level of control over the things that have happened to us, because, after all, no one event or series of events defines us – unless we let it.

> ### Reflection: Setbacks
>
> Consider an incident or period in your career which had a serious impact on your self-belief or confidence. The example is one of my own. Respond to the following prompts.
>
> ### What Happened? (in no More than three Sentences, Focused on *Facts*)
>
> **Example:** *I went for an internal interview during a restructure for a role at the equivalent level to the one I'd already been doing, happily and successfully, for*

a year. I prepared hard for the interview and loved the school. I didn't get the job and was effectively demoted.

What is the Dancing Gremlin* Saying?

*this is the voice which delights in self-sabotage and rubbing salt in the wound.

Example: I'm not cut out to be a senior leader. Everyone thinks I'm rubbish.

What is Empirically, Demonstrably True? If it was a While Ago, what Happened Next?

Example: The outcome was based on a points system. I was flummoxed by being interviewed by people I already knew and, if I'm honest, a little complacent. I was vague in lots of my responses, saying, 'well you know I did that – you were there!'

What have you Learned about Yourself from this Experience?

Example: I loved that school. I tend to let emotions rather than facts lead me – I belong here! I have so much to give. When being interviewed internally, it's best to pretend the panel are strangers. I was ready – and strong enough – for a fresh start.

For more on reframing, see Chapter 6 on limiting beliefs.

PEAK END RULE

The narratives we construct in our heads have far more power than *what actually happened*. As Strijbosch et al. put it, 'how individuals remember a certain experience may be just as important as the experience itself' (2019, p.1). The peak end rule or snapshot model (Fredrickson and Kahneman, 1993) is a useful lens through which to look at how we – and our colleagues – recall and recount their experiences in schools. This model suggests that how we feel about an experience is not based on the sum of its various components but is strongly influenced by how we felt at its peak or most intense point – and how we felt at its conclusion. This is helpful to us here because, however tumultuous or difficult a period has been, as colleagues and leaders of those departing our organisations – and indeed as individuals – we can influence the positive lessons and emotions that we and others take away from it.

Its function, according to Kahneman, is to help us avoid – or protect ourselves – from painful experiences in the future. It's related to the negativity bias (see Chapter 7) – our tendency to focus on the black spot on the white page; the one negative interaction or experience in an otherwise pretty positive day. By recognising this bias, we can take steps to enhance or emphasise our experiences – past and future – with fresh perspectives.

We can also capitalise on the power of endings by ensuring that all of our colleagues end their time in our schools with pride and dignity.

Reflection: Using Peak End Theory to Reflect on Your Career

Recall a period in your career that you remember positively.

- What was the most intense moment that you recall?
- How did it end?

Now do the same for a negative experience.

- What was the most intense moment that you recall?
- How did it end?
- How could you reframe the experience?
- What did you learn about yourself?
- What did the experience take from you?
- What did you *not* allow it to take away?

In my case, drawing upon the 'failed interview' account above, I remember the humiliation of the staff briefing the following morning when the results were announced, the less-than-dignified sobbing on the carpet of my colleague's office when I found out I'd been unsuccessful. But when I search through my memory files further, I also remember a certain young lady in Year 9 (that class which kept me awake at night, so volatile and unpredictable were they) running out of the gym with a large bunch of roses to give me on the day I left… Certainly a lasting 'peak-end' impression!

FOR LEADERS: PEAK END FAREWELLS

Here are some tips for school leaders on managing farewells in school settings.

Create a Memorable Peak Moment

- **Surprise celebration:** Organise a surprise celebration where students and staff gather to share their favourite memories and stories about the departing person. This can create a joyful and emotional peak moment.
- **Memory book:** Create a memory book filled with photos, messages, and drawings from students and colleagues. Present it during the farewell event as a keepsake.

End on a High Note

- **Farewell assembly:** Host a farewell assembly where students perform songs, dances, or skits dedicated to the departing person. This can be a fun and memorable way to end their time at the school.
- **Gift of appreciation:** Present a thoughtful gift that reflects the departing person's interests or contributions to the school, such as a personalised plaque or a framed photo collage.

Consider Individual Preferences

- **Quiet farewell lunch:** If the departing person prefers a low-key event, organise a quiet farewell lunch with close colleagues where they can share their thoughts and feelings in a relaxed setting.
- **Personalised playlist:** Create a playlist of the departing person's favourite songs and play it during the farewell event. This can add a personal touch and make the event more enjoyable for them.

Reflect on Positive Memories

- **Video montage:** Compile a video montage of clips from the departing person's time at the school, including highlights from events, classes, and interactions with students and staff. Show it during the farewell event to celebrate their contributions. You could also include personalised goodbye messages from colleagues and students.
- **Thank you cards:** Encourage students and colleagues to write thank you cards expressing their gratitude and sharing positive memories. Collect and present these cards as a meaningful gesture.

KNOWING WHEN TO SAY GOODBYE

In Chapter 6, we examined career trajectories with an emphasis on the fact that these will look different for each of us and, despite best-laid plans, will more-often-than-not be influenced by factors beyond our control, from life events to unexpected and exciting opportunities.

Making a judgement call on when it's time to say goodbye is no mean feat and, in most cases, nobody can make the decision for us. What's best avoided is what one colleague once called the 'witching corner' of the staffroom, full of people who feel harnessed to the school because of fear of change, financial responsibility, longevity or simply the fact that it's better the devil you know. Feeling 'stuck' in a role or school can lead to bitterness and eventually to burnout and is best avoided. And ultimately, life is short and we deserve to be happy – and whilst the choices will vary according to your role or location, we do always have choices...

Let's consider some of the factors you might consider when deciding whether to stay or go. I know many people with mantras they stick to: 'Three strikes and you're out' or 'If you wake up for four weeks in a row on a Monday dreading going to work, it's time to question your position!'

Reflection: When You Know You Need to Go

If you had a mantra or a definition of a 'red line' which means it's time to seek new pastures, what would it be?

If you're feeling disillusioned or frustrated with your current role, it's worth spending some time reflecting or talking it out with a trusted loved one or colleague. Writing down your frustrations in a secure space (without filter) can also be helpful.

Being really explicit about your boundaries is also powerful. Many people find it helpful to actively visualise these. Have a look at Figure 9.1 for the next reflection.

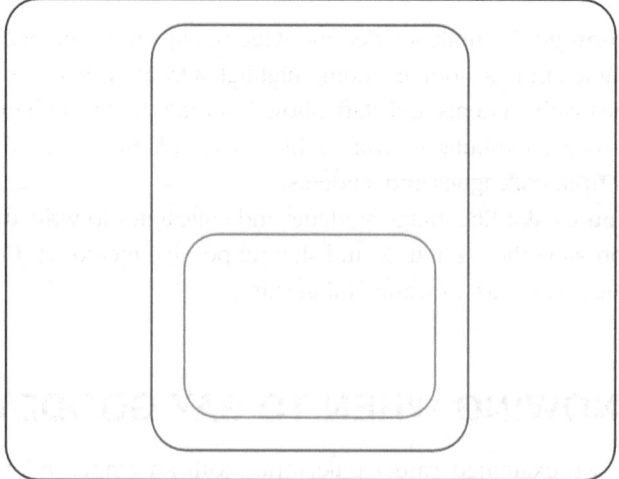

Figure 9.1 Your boundaries

Reflection: You and Your Boundaries

What elements of your role do you genuinely relish? What parts of it bring you joy? Jot these down (words or images) in the *central* rectangle.

For example: popping into colleague's classrooms and seeing and learning from brilliant moments; unexpected laughter with students...

Which elements that come as part of the package are you prepared to go along with, even if they might not always make your heart sing? Put these in the *middle* rectangle.

For example:analysing data, filling in essential paperwork, talking to angry parents…

And what are your 'red lines' – what behaviours, attitudes or expectations are you *not* prepared to bend for? (You might forgive these on one or two occasions, but if they're repeated, they'd make you seriously question your role). Put these in the *outer* rectangle.

For example: dishonesty, unfair practices, impropriety…

Now you've mapped out your boundaries, are there any other joyful, enriching activities you could seek out to fill the central rectangle? How might you do this?

How often do you find yourself having to step into the outer rectangle – into the no-go zones which clash with your values? If it's becoming a regular occurrence, it might be time for another context.

YOU AND YOUR WELLBEING AND WORK: REFLECTION AND CHECK-IN

With the caveat that everyone's priorities will be different, this reflection activity might help to offer some clarity if your feet are getting a bit itchy. N.B. This activity assumes that educators expect to work hard, that a reasonable level of stress is to be expected and can be managed and that young people aren't always angelic!

For this activity, consider the ten questions below. Score yourself on each question on a scale of 1–10, with 10 representing *as good as it could possibly be* and 1 representing *as bad as it could possibly be*. How would you score the following in your current role? As there are ten questions, your final 'score' will be out of 100.

1 I start my week feeling more optimistic than pessimistic.
2 My workload is rewarding and reasonable.
3 My stress levels are manageable.
4 I can balance work with my priorities outside school.
5 My students are engaged with their learning.
6 I am well-supported by leaders.
7 I feel valued and appreciated in my role.
8 I am happy with my opportunities for learning and growth.
9 My salary is fair and reasonable.
10 I have positive relationships with colleagues.

This isn't a teenage magazine (!) so the 'red line' here will be different for everyone – and the factors will carry different weights for different people. It may be that one single factor (e.g. a loved one needing care or an imminent financial commitment) will make your decision for you.

However, as a broad suggestion:

- If your score comes in at 35 or below, you may wish to start actively considering a fresh start somewhere else.
- If your score comes in at 65 or above, this suggests that, broadly speaking, your job is giving you much of what you need and want.

INVOLUNTARY DEPARTURES

It would be remiss of me not to acknowledge the hundreds (thousands?) of educators who leave their roles through no choice of their own. I was barely conscious of any redundancies in my first two decades of teaching but, with school budgets at breaking points, they are now a harsh reality for many schools, leading to eye-wateringly difficult decisions for school leaders (for which their training in no way prepared them). I have worked with educators brought to their knees by the most awful challenges, from formal questioning of their abilities and motives in the classroom to disciplinary issues to frustration at not having their talents and aspirations seen and met. We work in one of the few professions where, certainly here in the UK, the concept of 'innocent until proven guilty' is flipped on its head. I'm not sharing the link here because I don't want to draw attention to those named and shamed, but there's a website here in the UK where teachers and their alleged misdemeanours are named, with detailed accounts shared, *even if they were found entirely innocent of any accusations.*

Case Study: 'Mr D'

Innocent, but Removed

Mr D, a respected secondary school teacher in the South of England, was placed on 'gardening leave' after a vague safeguarding allegation was made by a student. With no prior issues and an excellent record, he expected a swift resolution. Instead, he spent over six months out of the classroom, isolated from colleagues and unable to access resources or defend himself while the investigation dragged on.

Though fully exonerated and found to pose no risk, the damage was done. His confidence was shattered, his role diminished, and whispers had circulated. He described the ordeal as 'the most dehumanising period of my professional life.'

This case highlights a harsh truth in UK education: when accused, teachers can be treated as guilty until proven innocent. Even when cleared, their names, reputations, and careers may never fully recover.

Mr D now works part-time and supports others going through similar challenges – quietly rebuilding, while carrying the scars of a system that failed to protect him.

Of course, due diligence is absolutely essential and robust processes must be in place to challenge unsafe and unethical practices, especially when young people are involved. This goes without question and should provide us all with a sense of security when it comes to calling out poor practice. But it doesn't always work like this, and I have seen educators brought to their knees by the questioning of their integrity, honesty and professionalism, sent on 'gardening leave' for months with little support and no clear answers, with catastrophic impact on their mental health and sense of self-efficacy. The tests to their resilience have been eye-watering, though it is heartening to say that the majority of those I've known (where there was no case to answer) have made fresh starts elsewhere to continue in the profession and their strength is humbling.

Whilst shinning a light into the murkier corners of our profession, it's also worth noting the phenomenon of 'disappearing' staff (in school one day, gone the next, never discussed or referenced by leaders again) and NDAs (non-disclosure agreements) – where staff are asked to leave quietly and never discuss what happened with anyone. Because these issues are, by definition, not discussable, a veil of darkness surrounds them and I believe this should give us all cause for concern in a profession that is founded upon growth and human capital.

WHAT KIND OF A GOODBYE DO YOU WANT?

As human beings, narratives are so important and colour the way we feel about key chapters in our lives. Whether heading off after a year or after decades, educators will have given so much of their very selves to a school, their colleagues and the young people that having a say in how they go is essential. For those of us lucky enough to have agency over our departures, it's worth considering, and communicating with key colleagues, what exactly we want. This will vary hugely according to life phases and contexts; when my kids were tiny, after a short-term contract, all I wanted to do was disappear quietly out of the back of the car park and be home in time for bedtime. When I left a school in my mid-twenties, I embraced the series of pub trips and picnics and lapped up the reminders of how much I'd be missed.

Case Study: Nancy

No Bells and Whistles, Thank You!

Nancy decided to retire after 38 years in her school, progressing from class teacher to headteacher, a role she'd held for the past 17 years. When I spoke to Nancy a few weeks before her departure, I asked her how she wanted her farewell to look. She looked a little surprised by the question and said she hadn't really

(Continued)

thought about it. As we talked, it became clear that she was hugely loved and that others were likely to miss her hugely, and these big feelings were likely to be reflected in any plans they made for her departure. Only Nancy is, in her own words 'quite an introvert'. She doesn't like being the centre of attention and very much sees herself as a public servant and someone who, with her characteristic quiet authority, enables others to do their jobs effectively. We concluded that it would be wise for Nancy to dial up her assertiveness on this occasion to ensure she had the kind of goodbye she was hoping for, rather than the bells and whistles and 'fuss' that would have left her flustered and embarrassed. In the end, staff were encouraged to come and see her personally. She said she really appreciated written notes but didn't want gifts, and during the leaving speeches, she, the site manager and the TA who were leaving all got equal attention, just as she wanted it.

THOSE LEFT BEHIND

It's a truism that nobody is irreplaceable, a lesson I learned relatively early in my career when I returned for a visit during maternity leave to discover, to my mild indignation (!) that the department was functioning just fine without me leading it and the new head of department was thriving, along with the rest of the team. However, everyone who departs leaves behind a unique them-shaped hole and the community will be subtly different for each staff member that leaves and joins. It's worth acknowledging, and planning for, the impact of the departure of a staff member. Obviously, this includes all the practical implications for ensuring their responsibilities are covered and training up any new staff, but there's also an undeniable emotional impact. This means the nature and flavour of the send-off can be as important for those being left as for those actually leaving. It also means considering how the less measurable, tangible roles that person performed are filled. If they were a confidant for staff, a hugger when things got rough; similarly if they were the one who didn't shy from the necessary but difficult conversations, if they had an eagle-eye for detail, or they knew the local community inside out, and so on, it's important to consider how those gaps might be filled. It's not an exaggeration to say I've seen staff grieve for a much-loved headteacher or teaching assistant and it's important, whilst not slipping on professional standards, to acknowledge that there might be some big feelings.

Case Study: Big Shoes to Fill

Nayla left after 10 years as a headteacher and was replaced by Patrick, an experienced head with many years' experience in a similar context. A few weeks after her departure, Nayla had plenty to occupy her, from her grandchildren, to her choir, to hill-walking. She valued contact with former colleagues, but she found she was being pulled back into school politics, which made things feel, in her words, 'messy and difficult'. Patrick, meanwhile, despite best-laid plans and preparations for his first 100 days, was made to run the gauntlet. 'Sometimes,' he said, 'I feel they hate me just for being not-Nayla.' He faced snide remarks, outright rebellion ('you don't get it – that's not how we do it around here') and was left bewildered and flummoxed in his attempt to build all-important relationships. By January, things had settled somewhat and he felt more accepted, but he remains staggered at the intensity of the emotion to which the replacement of beloved Nayla had given rise.

It was important too for Nayla to draw her boundaries and push back gently but firmly on attempt to get her involved with a reminder that she'd, quite literally, moved on, and that this must be respected.

TELLING THE CHILDREN YOU'RE LEAVING

Delivering the news to children and families is always, I'd argue, the hardest thing about leaving the school, and it's these moments that have stayed with me. I remember announcing my departure for maternity leave to an exclamation of 'What, Miss? You're having a baby?' from a certain 12-year-old (yes, Ali, it's not cake, I promise). He went on to suggest that I just brought the baby back in with me (which actually, I ended up doing on a number of occasions). On another occasion, I remember telling the tutor group I'd been with for four years that I was leaving – I'd seen them grow from bouncing frogs into gruffly-spoken young men; I'd seen them at their most vulnerable during family breakdowns and mental health crises, and at their most joyfully triumphant, in school performances and sailing in banana boats off the coast in the South of France. I remember feeling like the worst person in the world for abandoning them (and trust me, they don't sugar-coat it – 'what, Miss, are you saying the other school is better than us?'). The beautiful twist on this one is that a group of them rocked up 24 years later to wish me a happy 50th birthday. I remember leaving a school alongside over 30 staff after the most difficult year of my career. One student said, 'No, Miss. Not you as well'. I will never pretend this bit is easy, but this is where we must remember that, whilst it is quite probably the best job in the world, teaching *is* a job – never 'just' a job, but we are modelling important lessons to our young people in the way we leave and the accounts (which must always be professional) of why we have chosen to do so.

HANDOVER TIPS

The handover from a departing member of staff to the person or people taking over their role(s) is a crucial step in closing the loop and allowing for a clean departure. As well as the practical elements, explored below, it has metaphorical significance – if you're leaving, however fondly, you don't usually want to leave a part of yourself back in the classroom or office or need people to be calling you to track down key pieces of information when you've moved onto pastures new. If you can literally and metaphorically pass on the burden of responsibility in a systematic way, you can hopefully leave yourself not just with a clean break but with the last few days to truly enjoy the rituals surrounding your departure.

In offering the tips below, I'm somewhat boldly assuming that all the 'essentials' in terms of policies and procedures and expectations will be communicated centrally through a staff handbook and/or intranet, and instead focusing more on the elements that staff talk to me about... It's best to think about what the new person/people will want/need to know most urgently (and shelve what they can find out about as they go along, bearing in mind that brain-overload is a very real risk!). It's important to strike a balance between enabling them with key information and letting them go about the role with their unique strengths and a fresh pair of eyes.

Here are some key questions you might want to address, viewed through the lens of the person taking over:

Key Information

Where (exactly) can I find the key information I need to help me perform this role? For example, where can I find out about the needs of my class? Is there anything you can tell me about the children/colleagues that would be helpful to me? Where is the Scheme of Learning/Curriculum overview? What are the expectations in terms of balancing consistency with teacher autonomy when teaching, planning, marking, communicating, etc.? How far have colleagues/students got with ongoing projects/assignments and where are they?

Expectations and Success Criteria

What exactly does this role involve? Where's the job description and will it need adapting for me? What are the success criteria and who do I report to? What's been done already so I can avoid re-inventing the wheel?

Key People

Who are the people who will be able to support me in this role and what specific skills/knowledge do they offer? How and when can I access them if I need to?

Overcoming Setbacks

What challenges have you faced doing this role and how have you overcome them? What challenges do you anticipate me facing and what advice would you give me?

Systems and Accessibility

What devices(s) can I use and when? Where do I get my passwords (or retrieve them if I forget them)? Who do I go to if technology fails me?

TO AVOID! SOME LESS HELPFUL HANDOVER ADVICE

It's important that new staff (or staff taking over new roles) are armed with the information they need (e.g. if a parent has an ongoing grievance against the school or a staff member has been offered formal support in a key area). However, whilst it can feel helpful to 'pre-warn' them about challenges you have faced, it's also important to give them a fresh start and avoid giving them extra stuff to worry about in advance. Here's some less helpful handover advice I've received in the past and I'd suggest is best avoided as it causes lots of anxiety and didn't offer much productive advice:

'They probably won't like you as they were really attached to their previous teacher.'

'Watch out for her – you don't want to get on the wrong side of her!'

'They're a nightmare after PE on a Wednesday.'

'That unit is a nightmare to teach.'

CONCLUSION

Goodbyes in the teaching profession are deeply significant, marking the end of meaningful chapters and the beginning of new journeys. They offer opportunities for reflection, closure, and the celebration of contributions made. Whether through heartfelt farewells or quiet departures, the impact of these moments resonates with both the departing and those left behind. As educators, acknowledging and honouring these transitions helps us appreciate the profound connections and memories that shape our careers and lives.

REFERENCES

Armstrong, L. (1969). 'We have all the time in the world' [Recording]. www.youtube.com/watch?v=RMxRDTfzgpU

Burkeman, O. (2017). 'Consumed by anxiety? Give it a day or two'. *The Guardian*, 15 September. www.theguardian.com/lifeandstyle/2017/sep/15/consumed-by-anxiety-give-it-day-or-two

@CGSBucks (2024). 'Miss Thoday left CGS for the last time yesterday after 47 years to warm applause. *Wishing her a long and happy retirement'* [Post on X, 20 July]. https://x.com/CGSBucks/status/1814560483229200791

Fredrickson, B. L. and Kahneman, D. (1993). 'Duration neglect in retrospective evaluations of affective episodes'. *Journal of Personality and Social Psychology*, 65(1), 45–55. DOI: 10.1037/0022-3514.65.1.45

Goddard, V. (2024). 'My sister retired from teaching today after 38 years in the classroom in one school. No one from SLT spoke to her...' [Post on X, 19 July]. https://x.com/vicgoddard/status/1814401833030336652

Green Day, (1997). 'Good riddance. (Time of your life)' [Recording]. www.youtube.com/watch?v=CnQ8N1KacJc

Strijbosch, W., Mitas O., van Gisbergen, M., Doicaru, M., Gelissen, J. and Bastiaansen, M. (2019). 'From experience to memory: On the robustness of the peak-and-end-rule for complex, heterogeneous experiences'. *Frontiers in Psychology*, 10. www.frontiersin.org/journals/psychology/articles/10.3389/fpsyg.2019.01705

10

STICKING WITH IT

With this chapter, this book comes full circle. This chapter is about those who choose to stay in the job, those who choose to return, and the new colleagues who choose to join us. Although there's lots to be concerned about and systemic change is needed to attract and maintain the teachers our young people deserve, there is still always hope. A few years ago, I was working in a school where the all-important summer exam results were lower than expected and the challenges ahead for us were huge. Our headteacher showed us an image of a tiny wildflower growing through cracked concrete. This chapter, and the final notes of this book, remind me of that.

Teaching is tough and it's a job that not everyone is cut out for. In fact, arguably, it's harder now than it has been in (my) living memory to be a teacher or leader in a school. When I say these words to audiences of educators, there is rarely dissent. And, most often, there is a contagious glint that finds its way into the eyes of those in the room. As if to say, 'yes, it's tough. But *bring it on*. Because I've got the skills, the passion, the resilience and the tenacity to *make a difference*. As we learned from the wonderful teachers in Ukraine, sometimes it's during the toughest times that our sense of moral purpose resounds most powerfully. This is something that unites the hundreds of educators I have the privilege of meeting every year.

So, we can probably agree that the last few years have asked more of our educators than perhaps any other period in recent memory. And yet – despite the headlines, the statistics, and the challenges – there is always hope. Because, quite frankly, there has to be. Because young people will always need adult role models in classroom, i.e. teachers. I hold on to a *stubborn optimism*, forged over almost three decades in the classroom and countless conversations with teachers who, against the odds, are still standing, still laughing, still changing lives every single day with their compassion and dedication.

STICKING WITH IT: WHY SO MANY STILL DO

I've met countless teachers who've told me, quietly or defiantly, 'I nearly left.' Some did. Some walked away, took a breath, found themselves again, and later returned. Others stayed, clinging to the laughter of a Year 9 lesson that unexpectedly went brilliantly, or the moment a struggling student found their voice in a school play, or the message from a former pupil who says, 'You made a difference.' These are the moments that keep us going. They don't make the job easy, but they remind us why we do it.

Across the UK, as well as internationally, more and more schools and trusts are waking up to the fact that we cannot sustain our education system without looking after our teachers. I've worked with so many brilliant leaders who are prioritising staff wellbeing, building in flexible working, and rethinking what 'success' looks like. Schools where you can be a human as well as a professional, where it's no longer acceptable to glorify presenteeism or see burnout as a sign of dedication.

THE RETURNERS: A STORY OF RESILIENCE

Case Study: Katie

Rediscovering My Love for Teaching

I left teaching for the same reason a lot of people still are – I was burnt out. To a crisp. I had given it everything I had, late nights planning, marking, the stress of NQT observations and general lack of faith that what I was actually teaching was useful. I returned eight years later with one goal: enjoy yourself and don't go too hard. Now I love it. Supportive managers, strong boundaries (protecting my time) and not allowing myself to take work of any kind home means that I love it again, and so now I'm staying for the same reason I started. I really love teaching English.

Here's something I find particularly hopeful: the growing number of teachers who leave, and then choose to return. Data from the Department for Education shows that in recent years, thousands of qualified teachers who had left the profession have come back – in 2023–24, 8,210 former secondary teachers returned to teaching (Whittaker, 2024). Whilst it's a bud of hope, it does tell us something. Teaching gets under your skin and the rewards of the job make it worth reconsidering if you've left. And, despite the shrill cries of many on social media that an 'escape from the classroom' is the way forward, the grass really isn't always greener. This really isn't the hardest job in the world. In fact, I'd say it's frequently the most joyful – and the most important, and so goes the regular fierce debate with my journalist husband over whose job is more crucial!

Many of those who've left return with a renewed sense of purpose and boundaries that protect their energy and values. They've seen the world outside the classroom and realised that, for all its flaws, teaching remains a deeply meaningful profession. They've also seen the reality of reduced job-security and slashes to their take-home pay. I've spoken to returners who now job-share, work part-time, or have carved out new roles or 'fruit salad careers' that fit with family life and wellbeing. These aren't people who failed to cope – they're people who adapted, reset, and came back stronger.

THE STARTERS: THE ONES WHO STEP IN

Even now, amid all the noise and negative narratives about our profession, people are still entering teaching. And not just straight out of university; it includes, as we've discussed, career changers, parents returning to work, professionals bringing years of life experience into schools.

This is something I find genuinely inspiring. I remember a conversation with a newly qualified teacher who left a high-flying corporate job because, in her words, 'I got sick of making rich people richer – I wanted to do something real.' And she is – every single day.

Globally, the picture is both daunting and full of possibility. UNESCO estimates that 44 million teachers will be needed by 2030 to meet educational goals world-wide. That's a huge number, but also a huge opportunity – to rethink, rebuild, and reinvest in education as a force for global good. The work being done, for example by the OECD, is, I believe, profoundly refreshing and relevant, with its focus on what students and teachers will need to thrive and the use of a learning compass to help them navigate the world (OECD, 2024).

THE POWER OF HUMAN TEACHERS
IN AN AI WORLD

We hear a lot these days about the rise of AI. And yes, it's changing the landscape dramatically. But, with so many professions concerned for their 'replicability', I'd argue teaching is one of the few professions AI *can't* replace. Machines can mark papers and summarise content, but they can't build trust with a traumatised teen-ager, or spot the look on a child's face that says, 'I don't get it, but I'm scared to ask.' They can't improvise a lesson because the original plan just didn't land, or sit on the carpet with a tearful six-year-old whose morning hasn't started well.

Human intelligence, empathy, humour, intuition – these are what make teaching so uniquely powerful, and I genuinely believe real, human, adult role models will always be needed in learning spaces for children, however these might look in the years and decades to come.

In a world going through exponential, and sometimes terrifying, change, the importance of really listening to and engaging with young people is increasingly high on the agenda. A superb example of this is Rachel Higginson's 'Finding my voice' (2025) initiative, designed to empower young people by enhancing their oracy and personal development. Speaking to a group of teachers, Rachel makes the following powerful point, citing Klaus Schwab: 'We need to up our human-ness. We need to maximise the potential that this new era [the fourth industrial revolution] brings [...] We need to be powerfully human' (Culham St Gabriel's, 2025).

In times of conflict, climate anxiety, and economic uncertainty, young people need more than just knowledge. They need role models. They need adults who listen, who care, who model calm, compassion and resilience.

I've always believed that teachers are some of the most important stabilising forces in a child's life. In a turbulent world, the presence of a consistent, kind, and courageous adult can be transformative.

WHY I'M STILL HOPEFUL

I know the data. I read the reports. I see the headlines. I feel the frustration and the overwhelm. But I also see the teachers. I see the communities being built in classrooms, the creativity being sparked, the lives being changed.

I hold on to hope, not naively, but *intentionally*. Because I believe in this profession. I believe in the power of education to transform lives, and I believe in the people who show up every day to do just that.

To the ones who stay, the ones who return, and the ones who are just beginning: thank you.

I find myself coming another full circle as I end this book with the same message that I ended my first book, *How to Survive in Teaching*. In the words of Kevin McKellar, my dear friend and headteacher (may he rest in peace), let's never stop fighting the good fight.

Let's end with the voices of some teachers. I asked them on social media why they chose to stay in the profession. I received hundreds of responses, which was refreshing in itself. Here are a few of them.

WHY STAY IN TEACHING? VOICES OF TEACHERS

I'm a teaching assistant. I work in a small-ish school with wonderful teachers and fellow TAs, we genuinely look out for each other and it's a privilege to work with them. Every achievement of every child makes it worthwhile too, it just works for me.

Working with kids is really special. Teenagers are fun and surprising, and the job has so much purpose. My colleagues in my school are great and I love getting to work in the area I live in.

Because I love it. Every day is different, I'm never bored. The kids make me smile and I feel like I'm making a difference. Plus, I get paid to geek out about science every day! Yes, the workload is huge, but I can't see me ever leaving.

I'm staying in the job because I want to make a difference, no matter how small.

For the relationships I have made, am yet to make with every child or person. To believe in and remind them of who they are and all they can become. To model that kindness matters to others and themselves. Because It's a privilege to teach and I'm still learning daily.

Brilliant children. Nice atmosphere, Supportive colleagues & headteacher, Respect for my work. Freedom and autonomy to teach how I want. It's fun and rewarding. Musical. Not perfect, but pretty close!

If not me then who? I love doing it the majority of the time, find working with young people who are endlessly mind opening, inspiring and funny, and they need nurturing and support to enable them to become their best selves. I want to be part of that.

Working with children is life-giving! The workload is enormous but I can't imagine a better job.

Whilst at times challenging, with hugely long hours, I feel like I make a difference (I'm a cog in a fabulous team). Without effective education, many children will not reach their potential and have the life opportunities they deserve. I also love teaching (and challenge).

I feel so fortunate to work in Early Years, where we have developed our own curriculum and have some autonomy in what we prioritise (nurture). I work with a marvellous head, who ensures that our workload is manageable (as much as it can be) but is, above all else, kind.

I stay because I genuinely love my school. It has absolutely the right ethos and places staff wellbeing at the top of the SDP. I feel cared for and listened to (most of the time) and there is a real feeling of 'we're here to help make education a wonderful experience for all'.

The kids – they say 'thank you' all the time and they're funny. My current form group have made me one of those soppy teachers I (still) roll my eyes about – they're great. The senior leaders. The school values my subject (modern languages) and shows that consistently. I feel part of a team.

The pupils – they bring me daily joy. I have a laugh with them every day! Keeps me young.

REFERENCES

Culham St Gabriel's (2025). 'Oracy in RE. Do we need to talk more? 12 March. www.youtube.com/watch?v=6sCjz1pFSnM&t=4s

Higginson, R. with Awoyelu, E., Foley, C. and Myatt, M. (2025). https://findingmyvoice.co.uk

Organisation for Economic Co-operation and Development (OECD) (2024). *Future of Education and Skills 2030/2040*. www.oecd.org/en/about/projects/future-of-education-and-skills-2030.html

Schwab, K. (2016). *The fourth industrial revolution*. World Economic Forum.

Whittaker, F. (2024). 'Teacher recruitment could be worse than it looks, DfE suggests. Government forecasts "challenging period" ahead, will review NPQs, but there are record returners.' *SchoolsWeek*, 11 December. https://schoolsweek.co.uk/teacher-recruitment-could-be-worse-than-it-looks-dfe-suggests

INDEX